Love and Arms:
On Violence and
Justification After Levinas

Helen Douglas

Volume III:
Philosophical Psychology Series

Editor: Brent Dean Robbins

Helen Douglas

Love and Arms:
On Violence and Justification
After Levinas

Trivium Publications
Pittsburgh, Pennsylvania

Requests for permission to reproduce material from this work should be sent to Permissions, Trivium Publications, P.O. Box 8010, Pittsburgh, PA 15216.

Email: jhinfo@janushead.org

Cover designed by Nicole de Swardt

Sculpture on cover by Widus Mtshali

The extract from *Otherwise Than Being or Beyond Essence* by Emmanuel Levinas (Alphonso Lingis, trans. The Hague: Martinus Nijhoff Publishers, 1981) is reprinted by kind permission of Springer Science and Business Media.

ISBN 978-0-9713671-5-9

0 0 1 2 3 4 5 6 7 8 9 0 0

Other volumes of the Philosophical Psychology Series

Philosophical Counselling and the Unconscious Edited by Peter Raabe

Jung and Phenomenology By Roger Brooke

For Robert Sarginson, Mac Maharaj, and Andrew Feldmár

"There exists a teacher. One can perhaps learn to think."

I am the center of the universe —
I'm always here, if you want me

(Paul Durcan)

Contents

The works of Emmanuel Levinas are referenced in the text as follows

( ) *Otherwise than Being or Beyond Essence*

(¶1-15) Refer to the excerpt from *Otherwise than Being* (pp 157-162), see appendix

(AT) *Alterity and Transcendence*
- essays specifically quoted:
  "Philosophy and Transcendence", 3-37
  "The Proximity of the Other", 97-109
  "Peace and Proximity", 131-144

(EN) *Entre Nous: On Thinking-of-the-Other*
- essays specifically quoted:
  "The I and the Totality", 13-38
  "Useless Suffering", 91-101
  "Philosophy, Justice, and Love", 103-121
  "Diachrony and Representation", 159-177
  "Totality and Infinity. Preface to the German Edition", 197-200
  "Dialogue on Thinking-of-the-Other", 201-206
  "The Other, Utopia, and Justice", 223-233

(LR) *The Levinas Reader*

(OG) *Of God Who Comes to Mind*

(RPH) "Reflections on the Philosophy of Hitlerism"

(TI) *Totality and Infinity: An Essay on Exteriority*

Preface

The true problem for us Westerners is not so much to refuse violence as to question ourselves about a struggle against violence which, without blanching in non-resistance to evil, could avoid the institution of violence out of this very struggle.   *Emmanuel Levinas**

This is an attempt at such a questioning, written from South Africa in an uneasy time after the victory of the struggle against apartheid. Written, for that matter, after a century of victorious wars of liberation from colonialism, of revolutionary wars, of struggles against fascism, of violence committed in the name of justice and human rights: struggles against evil which have mostly failed to avoid the institution of violence, mostly failed to achieve the peace that was their deepest dream. It has also been a century in which non-violent resolutions to conflict were sought, both from within those conflicts, as oppressed people made use of the tactics of passive resistance and civil disobedience, and from without, as third-party bodies intervened to limit violence through negotiation, monitored treaties, and sanction. And yet violence fails to be contained. It is merely banal to note that the war to end war has not been accomplished.

Levinas's challenge is a crucial one for those - particularly those Westerners[1] - who would engage in a struggle against injustice. It leads directly to the paradox of just violence, and its consequences. An unequivocal American anti-war slogan of the sixties held that fighting for peace is like fucking for virginity. If one accepts the simile, and if peace is indeed the point, then one must decline to fight. But there is no peace if "good men" stand by and do nothing to stop the bad guys - bad guys fight to win. One question then, is, what is the significance of "the good fight"? Is there a difference between fighting for peace and fighting to conquer? If not, we're in serious trouble, seriously deluded, stuck in war until the bitter end, as if the best we could do would be to moderate our warfare, conduct it as "humanely" and as "reasonably" as possible. This is certainly not a bad thing, but efforts to contain violence also serve to keep its embers warm. If there is a difference, we need to figure out how to talk about it, and to think of a struggle that could consume itself - "such that from the ashes of this consummation no act could be reborn." (OB 185)

Another question concerns the peace for which the good fight contends. Will it indeed be virginal? Do we struggle for a peace like innocence? A wholeness or a purity, unbroken, unsullied, untroubled? This is not certain at all. We should question ourselves as well about the peace that may come as a spoil of war.

*   *   *

One day in May, 1987, two bombs exploded at the Magistrate's Court in Johannesburg. The first was a relatively small blast, and was detonated outside as an alarm, a signal to clear the building which, perhaps fifteen minutes later, was the target of the second and larger bomb. When the first one went off, two security force members were killed in the street.

That is the event as I remember it. I haven't bothered to dig back in the records of the day to fill in the details. The explosives may have been limpet mines and perhaps the first one was concealed in a car. I don't recall if the slain men were members of the police or the defense force. I can't tell you their names. I remember they were young.

At just that time, my husband and I arrived in South Africa to provide a safe house for the underground structures of the African National Congress. Prior to this, we had been active in the anti-apartheid movement in Canada. We had worked and become friends with many of the South African activists and exiles who passed through or settled in Vancouver. We had learned about the history of the liberation movements, watched the documentaries, read the books. From half the globe away we had, with righteous outrage, supported the armed struggle against apartheid.

The deaths at Magistrate's Court rendered that support of ours much less nonchalant, but they also deepened it. The evil of apartheid may have been simplified in its representation overseas, but it had certainly not been exaggerated. The need to fight back was not in doubt. Yet being here, suddenly involved more directly in this struggle, required a more thorough consideration of it. *Magistrate's Court.* Who were those two dead soldiers to me? What does it mean to kill an enemy at war? What does it mean to kill an enemy at war, when one has taken up arms in the name of liberation, freedom, justice? What does it mean, thou shalt not kill?

Nietzsche wrote, *He who fights with monsters should be careful lest he thereby become a monster.* I take this warning to heart, but notice: it is not the monster-fighting that worries him but the risk it runs. A freedom fighter should be careful. The evil of apartheid was - is - the evil that refuses to recognize the tender human dignity of another person. How can you maintain that you are fighting that evil if you in turn deny the humanity even of your enemies? And if you deny the humanity of your enemies, how would anyone be able to distinguish you from them, to distinguish your justice from their wickedness? A freedom fighter should be careful because armed struggle is an ambiguous and paradoxical act. But I cannot write that sentence without being interrupted by the bold exasperation of a poet - *Need I remind anyone again... that armed struggle is an act of love?* (Kgositsile 1990:25)

This is a strange thing to understand, but to try to sort through the contradictory threads of justification and violence should also be an act of love, or at least one which strives to be careful, to remain true, to not fall in with monsters. Nietzsche's aphorism concludes, "And if thou gaze into an abyss, the abyss will also gaze into thee." The poet calls us back at the abyss's edge, reminding us again, incessantly.

Chapter I. The Paradox of Just Violence

It is in a situation which is already violent and which compels a forceful response that the paradox of just violence arises. Justice first condemns and then demands violence, even to the point of killing. In violently resisting unjust violence, one finds oneself ethically obliged to do the wrong thing. This is a difficult position to sustain. The likeliest ways to resolve any consequent tension of conscience are to deny or diminish either the wrongness of the act or one's responsibility for acting, or to use the idea of justice as some kind of metaphysical agent which removes the possibility of censure for acts committed under its banner. In short, to rationalize an irrational situation. One says, *My enemy was a monster, not human.* And so, this killing was something other than murder. Or, *He only got what he, by his own actions, deserved - and anyway, he left me no choice.* And so he, and not I, is responsible for bringing about his own death. The metaphysically inclined just warrior can claim, *I am a soldier for the Good and therefore absolved from moral responsibility by this higher authority.* And so, for me, there is no problem. In short: I was justified to kill, to have done what would be abominable without that justification.

A fundamental dissatisfaction with this sort of thinking has been the impetus of this study. Rationalization seems to somehow miss the point. It does not take the ethical proscription against murder seriously enough and it depends too trustingly upon contingent social conventions and mores. Appalling acts of terror can also hide behind such claims of rational necessity. At the same time, the empirical criteria which have been elaborated for the determination of "just war" can themselves be shown to point to a deeper signification. Just war theory already assumes a real difference between justified and unjust violence, as though all that remains is to elaborate the rules of good conduct. What needs to be considered is whether separating the figures of just and aggressive violence does enough to address the paradox.

I will begin with a very brief discussion of justification as it appears in just war theory. There has been much careful and thoughtful work done in this field, but my aim here will be to just roughly sketch in the scene, just enough to indicate that something is happening outside or behind the picture, something that matters to us, something that will not be captured by filling in the scene with more and finer detail, and something, moreover, that is vital to the significance and meaning of the scene itself.

justification as fair play

The doctrinal determination of the justness of war relies on three conditions. Firstly, the cause of a just war must be just: it must be defensive, in response to a prior aggression; it must be taken up as a last resort; it must be openly declared and waged by a legitimate authority. Secondly, its conduct must be just: its violence proportional with that wielded by the aggressor, its targets limited to combatants. Finally, its intention must be just: the goal of just war is always the establishment of peace, and there must be reasonable hope of its achievement (Walzer 1977). These criteria suggest that aggression justifies resistance, that the justification of violent resistance exists within basic universal limitations, and that justified violence can condition the establishment of peace.

If we are to take up Levinas's challenge to question ourselves about a struggle against violence which avoids the further institution of violence, we may find a place to begin in this formal distinction between aggressive and resistant violence, that is, between unjust and just violence, and with the limitations of such justification.

The first suggestion of just war theory is that aggression justifies resistance. To aggress is to take the first step *(gradus)*, to attack or invade.[2] Aggression expands into another person, stakes a claim, proclaims privilege, proclaims a separate law unto itself which excludes its victim. By this same step, the other is then justified to resist *(re+sistere)*, to stand again. There is a sense that the justification of resistance serves to set things straight, put them *right*, to bring the aggressor back within the common law, by which law the one aggressed against is entitled - has a rightful claim - to defend his place, to self-defense. What is at stake is the righting of the wrong of invasion, the recuperation of a violated freedom, and the assertion of a law that is just in its equity and universality.

Justification acts with the force of the aggression, as if in accord with a classical physics where one action results in an equal and opposite reaction, or with the way a self-contained system attempts to regain a disturbed equilibrium. Aggression is an unwelcome incursion, an unjustified violence, an evil. Its force becomes the measure of return force that justification authorizes.[3] Justification suspends justice's condemnation of violence, but only conditionally: justified violence is still violence inasmuch as it befalls the aggressor without his or her full collaboration, inasmuch as it limits his or her freedom and imposes and enforces a non-autonomous law. The act of justification treats the aggressor's force as a proxy for the aggressor's collaboration, as if that action already included responsibility for what it provokes. The perpetrator is found to be responsible for the reactive violence he brings on himself. He brings reprisal on himself. Justification allocates his just deserts.

In this manner are retaliation and retribution justified. Retaliation is a simple *quid pro quo* exchange of hostilities. Retribution is a similar response authorized within the social system disturbed by aggression. Justification in these cases must concern itself with certain judgments. Equivalencies and equities will have to be established. Their justification appeals less to any ideal of justice than to calculations of justness, of pay-back, fairness and return value. Justice relies on justness, which justification measures and declares. As long as the force expended is within the limit of this measure, does not overspend or overtax itself, there is no reason for the one who deals out retaliation or retribution to ever feel a moral qualm. Justification removes the wrongfulness from the violence by adjudicating and distinguishing between the bad violence of aggression and the just violence of retaliation. The threat of bad conscience falls away.

And yet, it returns. Not merely as a worry that may we have miscalculated somewhere along the line, misjudged the situation: there is a also the strange fear that, even if we have stayed within limits set in perfect justness - if we believed such precision was possible - perhaps we have still gone too far, been too harsh. We worry that even this license hasn't put us in the clear. Not necessarily, of course. We may feel perfectly vindicated, perfectly in the right, perfectly at peace. What was wrong has been made right, and we have accomplished our duty, settled our accounts. And yet.

Retaliation is a limited and reactive violence, and so, better than aggression. Better, as well, precisely because it stands against aggression. And yet, we hesitate to depend upon it. If there were nothing wrong with this justified violence, why would anyone still cherish the idea of a non-violent resistance to evil? If the purpose of justification is merely to allow and to allocate the appropriate dose of homeopathic retribution required to cancel or correct for aggression, why does just war theory require that it be used only as a last resort? And even if we can dismiss the Sunday school admonition that "two wrongs don't make a right" by saying that retaliation isn't wrong, don't we fear that our retaliation may only escalate the violence, leading to the further justification of even greater force?

I have made no quarrel with the idea that aggression justifies resistance and that justification is limited to violence proportional to that of the aggression. These are indeed basic principles of the concept of just war. However, the force of aggression cannot be the only source of the limitations that govern justification.

justification as social warrant

The justification of retaliation or retribution must also be socially endorsed to be effective. It is not simply in the hands of the one aggressed against. It is bound by the conventions of approved violence and appeals more to these social contingencies than to any ideal of Justice, even if the former be mistaken for the latter. For example, since retaliation aims to effect a shift in relations of power from the aggressor back to the victim, its justification may be limited to conflicts between social equals. In such a case, retaliation against the aggression of a superior might not be declared justified (if indeed it was even recognized as aggression). In other words, retaliation assumes that the victim of aggression has the capacity within himself and his social position to pay back in kind. In addition, the victim may be expected to resist to the full extent of that capacity and can even be blamed for the aggression if he is found not to have done so. The flip side of this is that any merit that could accrue to the aggressor's case diminishes in accordance with the helplessness of the victim to resist.

Similarly, retribution is less the purview of the victim than of those who are entrusted to secure the ordered life of a community. The aggressor who challenges that order, who inserts himself into it by force, brings down retribution upon himself from on high. He is put in his place. Even if restricted to administering only a fit punishment for the crime, the superior is justified - declared righteous by rank - to use force against an aggressive interloper.[4]

The justification of retaliation and retribution is bound to reason as well as to law - or at least it wants its law to be as reasonable as it is forceful: logical, non-contradictory, well-founded, binding its subjects by its very rationality. If reason wants to appeal beyond social law for justification, it can do so by appeal to a natural law. It appears innate to human nature that we will seek to preserve ourselves and to defend against attack. From this, practical reason can take the necessary steps to declare self-defense to be a natural, universal and inalienable right for humans in community, a right which the law must then take account of.[5]

It remains the case that an act of retaliation considered separately from its origin must be a *prima facie* wrongful act - why else would there be need to return to it in order to elaborate a justification? Retrospectively, or in anticipation of retrospection, one is anxious to have this retaliatory act made right, declared to be righteous. Justification is that declaration. It clarifies the character of the violence of retaliation as justified, as an addition to that act. Justification is, in this sense, itself an accessory to violence.

The double nature of justification shows up in its etymology. *Jus*, that which is binding in its nature or character, such as righteousness, justice and law, combines with *facere*, which means both to do and to make. Justifying retaliation makes it righteous, declares it in accordance with the law.

Declaratory justification, as the authorization or legitimation or rationalization of resistance to aggression, as *making* righteous, goes back to the act, whether through law, custom or reason, in recognition of the resistance of aggression's target. The step of aggression steps over a line. The response of the one aggressed against will be judged in the context of that history and a certain legal code of rights and freedoms.

And yet. Can this be the full story of justification, if it still fails to capture the sense of justification of the *doing* right of resistance itself, within the moment of the act, as a work of justice bound beyond or otherwise than equitable legal justness, or of righteousness bound beyond or otherwise than rightfulness, a righteousness in the sense of Paul's *If righteousness come by the law, then Christ is dead in vain* (Gal. 2:21)? Can we ease apart the enigma of justification, try to find its beginning before the law was written, justification not of an act but of resistance itself, the being of human being answering for its being?

resisting violence: justification and being-justified

The sequence that structures declaratory justification starts with aggression, which gives rise to retaliation, which is then redeemed by justification. It takes as given that violence is wrong, but that defense is not as bad as offense. What makes the difference?

Declaratory justification is separate from the act it measures and is therefore later than the sense of being-justified of the one whose violence is judged. Self-defense comes naturally, including defense of one's place and property, of anything "one's own." It is right and necessary in its very moment, before any question of measured judgment. But only some such self-justifications will pass social muster - and every perpetrator feels justified in his actions at the time.[6] Again, what makes the difference?

It may be worthwhile to take a closer look at resistance as the common source of both justification and being-justified, of the wrong of violence and its vindication, the distinction between unjust and justifiable violence. Further, through questioning the phenomenon of resistance, we can become more precise about the nature of the wrong of violence, the relation of being-justified to justification, and the significance of the paradox of just violence.

Violence is an expression of strength. In aggression, its aim is to overpower - to establish power over - another. Such violence against persons is generally theorized as a violence against a freedom or the violation of a right. In this manner, I have spoken above of violence as that which befalls us without our full collaboration, which limits our freedom, or which imposes and enforces a non-autonomous law. But the wrong of violence, its evil, goes back not to abstract universals but to suffering.

In the preliminary discussion above, justification followed retaliation and retaliation answered aggression, but there is another interval. Resistance is what aggression meets. Resistance arises in the suffering of aggression. Aggression moves to take over the other's place and resistance takes a stand. Naturally. As a matter of course. Aggression meets a being intent on persevering in its being, a life living life, attached to its own interest, unable to yield to the aggressor and survive. Resistance to aggression is immediate and the necessary condition for retaliation. Retaliation is justified in the first place by the immediacy and irrefutability of this self-preserving resistance.

And yet, resistance is not always or exclusively self-interested. My resistance can join with yours in solidarity, an "us" together resisting a common aggression. And it can arise in defense of another, in non-indifference to another's suffering, as if that suffering was as immediate as one's own, as if one were already obliged not to leave that other one alone to his or her death. If the freedom of a "place of one's own" is the site of violation, and self-interested resistance is taken as the origin of justified and justifiable retaliation, it is not clear how these would allow for resistance and retaliation on another's behalf, in another's place. And clearly, we would want to include the defense of others as justified and justifiable. Indeed, one would struggle to justify the wrong of not coming to the aid of someone in distress.

It might turn out that the wrong of violence and the righteousness of resistance are not only matters of being and defending oneself. This would be a good thing, because if just violence only signifies as interested resistance to aggression, then there is nothing to prevent one just war from leading to another with the shifting interests that motivate aggression. Peace must be the goal of a just war, but the peace that follows a war of interests is unstable, a temporary containment of violence.

What is the wrong of a violence that is done to someone else, and how does it call for a response from me? In Levinas's words,

> These questions have meaning only if one has already supposed that the ego is concerned only with itself, is only a concern for itself. In this hypothesis it indeed remains incomprehensible that the absolute outside-of-me, the other, would concern me. But in the "pre-history" of the ego posited for itself speaks a responsibility. (117)

In the next chapter, I am going to elaborate Levinas's work more thoroughly, but what it suggests is that the wrong that aggression does to my neighbor is a greater violence than any violation done to my own freedom or being, a violation of another order to which I must respond, for which I am responsible. It is this "pre-historic" responsibility that first justifies retaliation, and it is an earlier justifying than the justification that rationalizes or legitimates after the fact. And moreover, it is a justifying that is precisely not a "self-justification", one which can not only survive the rigours of a retrospective judgment, but first requires such judgment.

Resistance to evil and aggression can say *Here I am*, and *Here I am for this other*, and *We shall not be moved*. The novelist Alice Walker has written that resistance is the secret of joy (Walker 1992:264). Resistance is joyous when it reveals or expresses a myself, an *I*, that is open, present and responsive, already involved with all the others. But resistance must act, and its actions always run the risk of falling into injustice, becoming monstrous. Resistance must submit to judgment - for example, by application of the criteria of a just war doctrine - but it is important to know, as Levinas frequently writes, whether that judgment seeks to curtail an eternal war of interests or to encourage an original responsibility which is signified in resistance to injustice.

Two senses of justification, one separate from the act and one active and immediate, led us to notice two resistances, one arising from one's own suffering and one from a concern for the suffering of another, which in turn suggested two conceptions of subjectivity, one for itself and one somehow responsible beyond itself. This of course brings us to Emmanuel Levinas, for whom everything that is human begins with the transcendent relationship of a subject to a radically and intimately exterior "other".

From Levinas's account of subjectivity as being-for-the-other, it may be possible to trace out another meaning to all these questions of the wrongs of violence, of justification and its risks, the significance of the "good fight" and the prospects for peace. This entry into Levinas - into fifteen paragraphs of *Otherwise than Being or Beyond Essence* (157-162)[7] - begins at the point where he has just asked, "Why know? Why is there a problem? Why philosophy?"

Chapter II. Reading Levinas

proximity: awakening-for

Levinas wonders what is at the beginning of a problem which, in seeking a resolution, finds itself caught up in questions about truth, reality, cognition, language and meaning - in other words, produces philosophy. He will resist the notion that this consciousness is simply how humans are, that we are bound by an insignificant "anonymous law of the 'human forces' governing an impersonal totality." (¶14) Rather, he finds that consciousness comes out of *proximity*, out of a subject's relation with and responsibility for an other. Proximity becomes knowing and remains the "signification of the very knowing in which it shows itself." (¶1) A problem that calls for knowing begins, latently, in proximity.

Proximity is the relation at the heart of Levinas's philosophy, and the most slippery to define in all its branching out. Here is how Levinas sums it up at the end of *Otherwise than Being or Beyond Essence:*

> Signification, the-one-for-the-other, the relationship with alterity, has been analyzed in the present work as proximity, proximity as responsibility for the other, and responsibility for the other as substitution. (184)

Proximity is a relationship with alterity: a metaphysical "relation without relation" (TI 80).[8] The otherness of alterity is not simply difference, which would still refer to a system or an opposed identity that I could grasp or comprehend. Alterity is profoundly a "not-me", a radical exteriority beyond any system. And yet, it has something to do with me. In the relation of proximity, in the approach of this otherness, I am concerned immediately, without mediation.

Proximity, the approach of the other, can be compared to being woken from a sound sleep. Suddenly, in the perfect darkness and silence of the night - with a shock - you awake. You are this heart that pounds, these eyes and ears that strain towards . . ., this "me" that finds itself whispering: *yes?* You find yourself torn from sleep, not by an impersonal wind that rattles the window, or by the neighborhood dogs that disturb everybody within earshot, or by the shouting laughter of late-night revelers who don't care whose sleep they trouble. It is as if you were called, as if this call came rightfully to find you, you and no one else, as if your vigilance was urgently required. A call which echoes silently within you in your awakening. An appeal whose only trace is found now in your own presence, your own response. *Yes?*

It is an uncanny experience. Levinas calls it revelation, the passing of the Infinite.[9] What is revealed? Not the one who has called - there *is* no one *there*, except perhaps enigmatically in the fact that the response to it takes form as a question that is anything but rhetorical, as a petition or prayer[10] that is directed towards..., and waits, breathlessly, for a reply. "Here there is an inversion of order: the revelation is made by him that receives it, by the inspired subject whose inspiration, alterity in the same, is the subjectivity or psyche of the subject." (156) The revelation is made by the one who has received it, the one who begins passively as only this naked response, troubled or besieged or obsessed by this otherness that is strangely, even abusively, within. What is signified in proximity is a subject who responds: a subject, uniquely and irremissibly *I*, who is responsible to this other, who is the place of the other, and who takes that place as a substitution for the other.

Those who are familiar with Levinas may be wondering that I use *"yes?"* for this first saying of subjectivity. It is, to my ears, more in accord with his *"me voici"* than is the standard English translation of "here I am" which often seems to be too bold, too declarative for the stripped and passive subjectivity of proximity. "Here I am" may be mistaken as an assertion of locus, egoic subjectivity and being. *"Me voici"* is perhaps just a step before that: *me*, an accusative rather than subjective pronoun, the object of a "seeing" *(voir)* that has found me here *(ici)*; a "here" that is first of all only relative to the distance this seeing has traversed.[11] "Here I am" is apposite in proximity - if at all - only as a reiteration of *"yes?"*, of *"me voici"*.

I have also intentionally avoided Levinas's "face-to-face" in my metaphor of proximity as being-awakened. In this instant of proximity (which is only an "instant" for the awakening or saying subject and does not include the other whose presence is already past or yet to come: the instant is not synchronic, but diachronic), it is important to hold to the fact that there are no faces visible here. What Levinas calls the Face of the neighbor is, in proximity, a non-phenomenon. "It escapes representation; it is the very collapse of phenomenality. Not because it is too brutal to appear, but because in a sense too weak, non-phenomenon because less than a phenomenon." (88)

If there is a confusion here about the form or formlessness of the neighbor and the neighbor's face - some avoidable confusion, that is, apart from its essential ambiguity - this may again come back to translation. In French, the other who ap-proaches in proximity is the *proch-ain,* the nearest. In English, the *prochain* becomes the "neighbor" which is fine if taken back to its archaic roots as "one who dwells nigh" but is a problem if taken in its more determined modern setting as "a person who lives near another", or one who could be loved "as oneself". In the instant of proximity, of the ap-proach of the nearest or nighest, there are no faces visible. There is not light enough, nor space. I am responsible to the Other, I respond as the unique one ordered or chosen before any question of visibility or recognition - is this my neighbor? - could arise.

Levinas says that proximity *orders* me to the other. I am ordered in all the meanings of the word. To order is at once to give arrangement to, to command, and to ordain. The other is before me, not as in a spatial arrangement of entities present together but because the other precedes me, was "the first one on the scene" (11); I find myself under orders, my allegiance pledged already in my response; and I am ordained to the other, assigned uniquely as if by decree or destiny. Proximity orders me to the other across an infinite interval, in a relationship so intimate as to allow not even the breadth of a hair to be inserted between me and this other. Proximity produces the unmediated responsibility of the one-for-the-other.[12]

My response - *yes?* or *me voici* - is an approach towards that which has both found me and obsessed me. My response opens the door from my side, welcomes the other. And then, and there, I find that proximity has not "ordered to me only the other alone" (¶ 2). My venture out towards this other before me brings before me all the other others, all humanity, or "the third party" as Levinas terms it. "The way leads from responsibility to problems." (¶13)

proximity and the third

Responsibility up to this point might be said to be completely "mindless". The one-for-the-other is not a commitment or intention, not freedom or non-freedom: it is a modality of passivity. Prior to any world, it signifies the "anachronous birth, prior to its own present" (139), of the subject.

This responsibility brings me before the third party which "introduces a contradiction in the saying whose signification before the other until then went in one direction." (¶3) Consider the variations of relationship that Levinas presents in this paragraph:

- The third is "other than the neighbor, but also another neighbor".

As I follow in the trace of the proximate other - who has approached me and to whom I am ordered - that other withdraws, "before and beyond", as if my responsive approach augmented the distance between us, indefinitely and infinitely. What does appear before me, visibly, is *the third party:* other than the neighbor, but also a neighbor, precisely when the face of the third breaks through its plastic appearance to express the command and appeal that have already ordered me and which order me *as well* (equivalently, without distinction) to this one who now faces me - my neighbor.[13]

- ". . . and also a neighbor of the other, and not simply his fellow".

This means that this third is responsible for and ordered to the other in proximity, without reference to me. Insofar as this is between them, it is not my business. They are something to each other before they appear to me as fellows, as two of a kind. Because of this relation between them, I cannot entirely answer for the other, "even if I alone answer, before any question, for my neighbor." This problem that appears with the entry of the third, this "limit of responsibility", will be the constraint of the subject-in-proximity necessary for the foundation of consciousness.[14]

- "The other and the third party, my neighbors"

The entry of the third party has two consequences. The first is that the Other, without splitting or diminishing or duplicating itself in any way, becomes many, becomes different others. In place of the-one-for-the-other, two unique terms related in proximity, one has "neighbors". It is as if the Other of proximity accomplishes something like a substitution of its own, puts the others in its place, in one's way. Alterity turns up as difference, even as it continues to overflow any notion or particularity of difference. My approach to the Other, *yes?*, diverted without changing its aim, brings me into the presence of the visible faces of all the others.

- "my neighbors, contemporaries of one another, put distance between me and the other and the third party."

The second consequence of this entry is the establishment of discrete space and synchronic time, again because of the relation between the others that already complicates my situation: but it is precisely this complication which opens for the subject the spatial and temporal planes necessary to take a stand or gain a perspective.

In all of these relations of proximity, the latent subjectivity exists only as a passivity, a response that takes place as substitution, as the-same-for-the-other. It is the "chosen one", obsessed by the other, held hostage, persecuted without a freedom or choice it could call its own. It arises as responsibility, already responding to and answering for its separation from the other, only through the withdrawal of the other. This paradoxical withdrawal that does not sever its relation Levinas names *illeity*. It signifies the passing and the command of the Infinite which

> orders to me the neighbor as a face, without being exposed to me, and does so the more imperiously that proximity narrows . . . This way for the order to come from I know not where, this coming that is not a recalling, is not the return of a present modified or aged into a past, this non-phenomenality of the order which, beyond representation affects me unbeknownst to myself, "slipping into me like a thief," we have called *illeity*. It is the coming of the order to which I am subjected before hearing it, or which I hear in my own saying. It is an august command, but one that does not constrain or dominate and leaves me outside of any correlation with its source. No *structure* is set up with a correlate. Thus the saying that comes to me is my own word. (150)

The commanding order of illeity orders the order of proximity, which is the order of Same and Other where the separation between them is a relation between an alterity and an "I" whose interiority is not its own, the infinite in the finite, until the other arrives before me in the face of my neighbor. Proximity begins "becoming knowing" (¶1) enigmatically, here in the "dawn of a light which proximity changes into" (ibid.), expressed in the revelation of the face-to-face.

It is important not to move too quickly at this liminal point of the analysis. The face is still not yet visible, does not yet appear. Proximity does not light up the planes and surfaces of a face open to one's vision and discernment. Its resonance is first the light that "is needed to see the light" (TI 192), a unique "resonance of silence" (30).

Proximity as the order of Same and Other is like a bridge between the non-phenomenality of illeity or alterity and the various tangibilities of the order of being and beings. Its only modality is passivity, responsibility, the one-for-the-other. It is an impossible responsibility, both unassumable and indeclinable. When Levinas writes that there would be no problem "[i]f proximity ordered to me only the other alone" (¶2), this should not be taken to imply or guarantee a trouble-free life if only the other and I could be alone together in the world. Let me insist again: proximity is exactly *not* being, *not* together, *not* in the world. The other will indeed turn to show me a face, but that is already on the "other side", after the turn to being. Proximity signifies as responsibility: it is problem-free because of the immediacy of the relation with the other, "an immediacy antecedent to questions" (¶2). No questions, no consciousness, no problem. "It is troubled and becomes a problem when a third party enters." (ibid.)

falling into being: contact, sensibility, exposure

Levinas's accounts of the passage between the orders of proximity and being tend to describe the interruption of being by the alterity of the other. The self-referral of the subject's identity, the subject's complacent return to itself in identity and self-consciousness, is catastrophically called into question by the revelation of the face.

Because it is posed - even imposed - by the other who faces me, the question is an ethical one: "the breakup of essence is ethics." (14) The rhetorical difficulty that arises here is that the language of ethics is then carried back in discourse to the relation found in proximity, risking certain misdirection because *there is certainly nothing ethical about proximity.* Nothing to question, nothing at all. To speak of persecution and hostage-taking and violation in proximity is excessive, forcing the philosopher to incessantly refute that there is any freedom or intent or will at work, lest the straightforwardness of proximity ossify into a morality or ideology. If the language of ethics nevertheless remains appropriate to proximity - and it does - this only bears witness to the weight of being that discourse, the Said of the philosopher, necessarily carries back toward proximity, toward the anarchic order of the Saying of the *I* that is the original impulse of language.

Another approach of discourse to proximity would be to judiciously complement or compensate Levinas's excesses by trying to follow proximity every step of the way as it reverts or drops into being, to resist the solecistic use of ethical language until it becomes irresistible in the breaking and binding of the face-to-face, in the transilient moment before a face that shows itself "between transcendence and visibility/invisibility" (¶5).[15]

Here is a description of that moment from *Totality and Infinity:*

The face with which the Other turns to me is not reabsorbed in a representation of the face. To hear his destitution which cries out for justice is not to represent an image to oneself, but is to posit oneself as responsible, both as more and as less than the being that presents itself in the face. Less, for the face summons me to my obligations and judges me. The being that presents himself in the face comes from a dimension of height, a dimension of transcendence whereby he can present himself as a stranger without opposing me as obstacle or enemy. More, for my position as *I* consists in being able to respond to this essential destitution of the Other, finding resources for myself. The Other who dominates me in his transcendence is thus the stranger, the widow, and the orphan, to whom I am obligated. (TI 215)

To *posit oneself* as *I, able* to respond, *finding resources:* how does this sudden agency arise? It is effectuated in the crisis of responsibility, in "the non-postponable urgency" (TI 212) with which the other requires a response and the impossibility of fulfilling that responsibility.[16] The tension is enigmatically resolved by the presentation of the face of the neighbor in the light of proximity, which is the furthest reach of proximity toward the order of being. Enigmatically, because ambivalently. *Something happens*, but the resolution is never accomplished. Proximity does and does not coincide with subjectivity. Levinas writes that subjectivity, "prior to or beyond the free and the non-free, obliged with regard to the neighbor, is the breaking point where essence is exceeded by the infinite. It is the breaking point, but also the binding place; the glow of a trace is enigmatic, equivocal." (12) Coming the other way, it is within the face that the infinite somehow falls into essence, as substitution or becoming, as a summoning and a judging, by way of "the being that presents itself. . . without opposing me as obstacle or enemy."[17]

In proximity, in my saying addressed to the other, like a supplicant I am exposed. "Here I am" without the wherewithal of being: as "a latent birth, [the subject] is never a presence, excluding the present of coinciding with oneself, for it is *in contact,* in sensibility, in vulnerability, in exposure to the outrages of the other." (139) These are the immediacies of subjectivity, attendant at its beginning.

To be in contact is not to grasp, but to be grasped, "not an openness upon being, but an exposure of being." (80) Sensibility is not first of all the experience of a sensation, but the unity of the sensing and the sensed in the vulnerability and exposure of a skin. Before pain and pleasure, the immediacy of sensibility is "the ease of enjoyment, more immediate than drinking." (64) As enjoyment, exposure to the other is a plenitude or contentment, the relief of being met in a rendezvous in which neither the self nor the other is suppressed. Sensibility in proximity - and here we are very close to the line, yet still earlier than ego - is the common beginning of animation and incarnation. From the beginning of its rememberable time, the egoic subject will find itself possessed of body, heart and mind as a personal interiority but in the anarchic diachrony of proximity, psyche signifies the one-for-the-other, and soul the-other-in-the-one, already signifying subjectivity as obsessed by and for the Other, a "passivity of the for-the-other in vulnerability, which refers to maternity, which sensibility signifies" (71).

Levinas would have it that pain and wounding arise "at the same time" as enjoyment (64), but I think I must take issue with him here. He speaks of "a coring out *(dénucléation),* . . . a non-coinciding of the ego with itself" (ibid.), a "pain" or "vertigo" that confounds the ego "when it posits itself in itself and for itself" (ibid.). Again, this refers to a breakup of the essence of subjectivity by the other. Levinas is describing an awakening-from. My evocation of proximity, on the other hand, begins with an awakening-for prior to the susceptibilities of a self-identified ego. This is obviously an intentional act on my part, and therefore disingenuous at least, but since the awakening in a way inaugurates diachrony, it seems that a reduction that brackets egoity is not necessarily inappropriate. Active, intentional, egoic subjectivity is a condition of an analysis of proximity. It is not, however, a condition of proximity, that is, of "proximity, which is not an "experience of proximity" (76), nor of sensibility, which is not an experience of sensibility.

Does proximity then not immediately expose me, as Levinas has it, "to the outrages of the other" (139)? I am not suggesting that at all. This call that comes to call me from my rest in whatever still darkness, that provokes my response - *yes?* - and my responsibility or non-indifference, that both concerns me and withdraws from me, that impels me to exposure and vulnerability in my own voice: of course it is outrageous, but perhaps not in the sense of an insult or a violation, but rather as an extravagance, excess, luxury. The word outrage derives from *ultra:* beyond + *rabere:* to rave, to be mad. I, in the accusative, me alone, am exposed and vulnerable to this relentless, raging and delirious forcefulness from I know not where, from beyond. Any one of us (as onlookers, from some outside perspective), might well object to the pain of a *someone* unwillingly torn up in such a ravishment, but in proximity this exposure to gratuitous outrage is the way that the enigmatic and unique relation of the *I* and the other comes to pass in a transcending diachrony. "[T]hat the Infinite comes to pass there, is what makes the plot of ethics primary, and what makes language irreducible to an act among acts . . . saying is witness; it is saying without the said, a sign given to the other." (150)

falling into being: as the Other turns

This survey of the immediacies of proximity has been a bit like a stage magician's overture to a conjuring. "Ladies and gentlemen, please observe carefully: there is nothing up my sleeve, and this box before me is indeed completely empty!" The task now at hand is to bring to the stage the third party whose apparition "is the very origin of appearing" (¶10) and who opens the exigency for justice and hence justification. But first there is the final liminal moment whereby the subject, from the first, is enabled to take on the possibility of possibility in response to the "face with which the Other turns to me" (TI 215). The face is enigmatic. It is the gateway between proximity and being. It acts on either side of the divide, or both, in its own way another breaking place and binding place, at once abstract and concrete to knowing.

Moving from proximity toward being, "the being that presents himself in the face comes from a dimension of height, a dimension of transcendence whereby he can present himself as a stranger without opposing me as obstacle or enemy." (ibid.) This is still not a representable presentation. "A face obsesses and shows itself, *between* transcendence *and* visibility/invisibility." (¶5, my emphasis) It effects a crisis for the I, unique and irreplaceable, that is already penetrated by the other, already responsive, already in contact, already open and exposed.

The face that turns toward me is a reduction of the other "reduced to having recourse to me" (91). It is "a trace of itself, given over to my responsibility." (ibid.) All of the immediacies of proximity - response, contact, exposure - coincide with this offering from the other, this giving over of a trace of itself to my responsibility, given over to me "in trust". This recourse to me, "the homelessness or strangeness of the neighbor . . . is incumbent on me." (ibid.) It lies upon me like a weight, a burden that I have no capacity either to bear or relinquish, to request or refuse. And yet I am subjected to it. This turning of the face to me is the outrage within the relation of proximity, the exposure to the other that wounds. It is not an ego that is unable to return to itself, but a latent subjectivity, not present to itself but in proximity with an Other, in the immediacy of enjoyment, that is exposed to a face that turns to me and "summons me to my obligations and judges me" (TI 215).

This burden, this incumbency, is my subjectivity. I am for the other, compressed or contracted into myself, putting myself in place of the other as a hostage, positing myself as an *I* in responsibility, ordered to respond, to find resources for myself, and "to give to the other taking the bread out of my own mouth, and making a gift of my own skin." (138) Levinas calls this adventure *substitution*.

In substitution, subjectivity signifies the-one-for-the-other. Substitution is the origin of signifying. This is not an act of exchanging places. It is a hyperbolic passivity, an exposure that holds nothing in reserve, an exposure of exposing. I take up an identity as an I, which is not a self-recurrence, but occurs in the impossibility of escaping my subjection before the face of the other. This *I* is not "an ego", one among many. It is not generalizable. It is something like a verbal pronoun without a noun, being-I before being a being, being "bound to others before being tied to my body" (76). I am who says I. I am exposed in my saying, prior to anything being said. Exposed to the other for whom, and on whose command, I am saying. I am identified by the accusation of the other. *Me voici*. I identify myself in that exposure and expose it again. "[S]aying is witness . . . a sign given to the other." (150) Here I am.

the epiphany of the face

The Other turns toward me a face to which I find myself obliged, a face that is enacted as sovereign to my subjectivity, but what is the nature of this obligation? Levinas records the "primordial expression", the first sign or saying of the other given to me, as "you shall not commit murder." (TI 199) Again, I would like to slow this down. There is no question of murder in proximity: the vulnerability to exposure is not yet the vulnerability of any body. The face gives over a trace of itself as destitution to my responsibility, but it is not given as a phenomenon.[18]

The expression of the face calls me to attention, calls me to order, calls to me alone, elected, unique, irreplaceable in my responsibility to this call. I alone can respond. I, *qua I*, am-for-the-other. Subjectivity, oneself in proximity, is a null-space, is substitution, is signification, witness, a sign given to the other before the other appears in any way to consciousness, a sign given or torn away in a passivity prior to any freedom.

To be for-the-other is not to take the place of the other. The relation of proximity - in which the Same is separate from the Other, and the otherness of the Other is not difference but alterity, a radical exteriority - is not collapsed by substitution. Responsibility is "a substitution in separation." (54) I do not fuse with the other but am opened to my depths, to myself, to my identity as unique before the other. By the appeal of the face that the other turns to me, the enigmatic presentation from "on high" of a being reduced to recourse to me, I am myself contracted in substitution into being. Inspiration changes into respiration in the final breathless moment of proximity's imminent reversion into being, as much an exasperation as an expiration.

Responsibility is unexceptional. Proximity is peace. And then I am ordered to myself, to be for-the-other, in the epiphany of the face. Psyche, the one-for-the-other, is my approach to the other in proximity, but proximity is suddenly - in the urgency of my responsibility - never close enough. By my very identity, by my occupying the arena of being, I repel and send away the other, the neighbor. My every approach rends the peace and I must then re-establish it. (137) "Peace with the other is first of all my business." (139)[19]

This, if I have been attentive enough, will be the first entrance of the language of ethics into an analysis that moves from the order of proximity toward the order of being. The approach of the other in proximity calls me to responsibility: a call which is not alienating because it comes to me in my own voice, and an asymmetric responsibility which goes from me to the other without reciprocity. My presence is required - and yet I always find myself too late and the other already distanced by my arrival. Responsibility reverts into a persecution. I am held hostage for the other, ordered to make expiation for a fault that I could not avoid, in an unavowable innocence. To make expiation, even for my own being, is to make peace with my neighbor, the one most nigh. "Peace is incumbent on me in proximity . . . I am a hostage, for I am alone to wage it, running a fine risk, dangerously. This danger will appear to knowing as an uncertainty, but it is transcendence itself" (166-7). The other first addresses me not in an injunction against murder, but in a plea for peace - a peace to which I am called as uniquely responsible.

This is not at all an account of original sin, but of the "original goodness of creation" (121). Responsibility, substitution, and goodness are prior to freedom or choice or violence in the subject. It is important to understand this priority. It is not that proximity precedes being in measurable or memorable time or that it is a condition or foundation upon which being is erected. It is not that I "am" responsible or good - as though it were a quality for which I could congratulate myself. It is not voluntary. Goodness chooses me first. To be for the other, to say, to expose oneself, is already goodness. But it is not an action taken up by an agent, willing or unwilling. In the passivity of the same in proximity with the radical alterity of the other - this unique relation - infinity comes to pass. Subjectivity is diachronic, born "out of synch", bearing a trace of a beginning without foundation, a creation *ex nihilo* immediately in approach to the transcending other, subjected to election and responsibility. As the other turns a face to address me, I am for-the-other, psyche and soul, hostage and substitute, bearing the other in a figure like maternity.[20]

the appearance(s) of the third party

The face does not only reveal or expose the subject in relation to the infinite. In another movement of the presentation, the other also immediately exposes me to all the others. "The third party looks at me in the eyes of the Other . . . It is not that there first would be the face, and then the being it manifests or expresses would concern himself with justice; the epiphany of the face qua face opens humanity." (TI 213)

Again, one must travel very slowly here. "The apparition of a third party is the very origin of appearing, that is, the very origin of an origin." (¶10) The apparition of the third is indeed a phenomenon, the appearance of someone "before my very eyes", but it is a someone who obsesses and commands and appeals to me. He is not reducible to the theme in which he shows himself to my gaze because he bears in his face the trace of the unthematizable otherness of proximity to which I am already bound. He does not appear for my use or my pleasure or to oppose me, but from within the bond of my responsibility. But he is at the same time a "third party" because he intervenes in the interval of proximity between the Same and the Other. The third party *is* my neighbor.[21] He is the nearest other, reduced to recourse to me, the one who "can present himself as a stranger without opposing me as obstacle or enemy." (TI 215) This is the one for whom peace is required, for and before whom I am answerable.

Through illeity, out of the signifyingness of subjectivity in proximity which signifies as the one-for-the-other, my neighbor presents himself to me, but I am at the same time exposed to the faces of others as well. Any or each of these faces, inasmuch as it bears the trace of the Other, may break in upon me as an appeal or command to my responsibility and resources which until then went only from me to my neighbor.

The third party interrupts the immediacy of proximity. If proximity is peace, can we then charge the third with breaking the peace? Levinas says we cannot: "it is because the third party does not come empirically to trouble proximity, but the face is both the neighbor and the face of faces, visage and visible, that, between the order of being and of proximity the bond is unexceptionable." (¶10) My relation with the third party, my neighbor, through his face, is both a relation in proximity and in the order of being, but I am already bound to him before I recognize him in his features. That he appears as someone before me does not collapse that allegiance. On the contrary, it is from that allegiance and obsession that I am compelled to search his face, to question his situation in the world and in regard to myself. It is because he looks at me that I must look to myself.

Prior to any freedom or choice of mine, and coming to me as if in my own voice, the approach of the other in proximity finds me and commands my response. I am awakened to myself for the other. This awakening in contact is immediately the sensibility of enjoyment, and substitution: being-for-the-other and the maternal bearing of the other, being penetrated by and burdened with "the absolutely other, the stranger whom I have 'neither conceived nor given birth to'" (91). To be a subject is to be subjected-to, exposed in a hyperbolic passivity that can not be assumed, a passivity beyond patience "more passive than all passivity", as Levinas regularly writes.

The for-the-other of proximity is substitution, is saying, is being exposed as *I*, a sign given to the other. The other turns to me a face. In its first moment, I am contracted into myself, too late on the scene and too distant, obliged and determined to reconciliation with my neighbor, to expiation for him. This is not an alienation. Very simply, it's what I - as *I*, not as *cogito* or *conatus* or ego, but as just this unique and incomparable subject, in contact with this unique and incomparable other - do. *Me voici*. Here I am, subjected and accused in an infinite responsibility, in the "original goodness of creation".

The third party, my neighbor, appears in a second moment of the face, "looking at me in the eyes of the Other", "both visage and visible". My simple response to the other is insufficient here. The neighbor requires more than passive attention and exposure. In this light, we can return to the command that Levinas ascribes to the first expression of the other.

> Responsibility for the other - the face signifying to me "thou shalt not kill," and consequently also "you are responsible for the life of this absolutely other other" - is responsibility for the one and only. The "one and only" means the *loved one*, love being the condition of uniqueness. (EN 168)

The appearance of the neighbor is the exposure of his vulnerability to me, a vulnerability that is my concern both through his appeal or accusation, and also through my trepidation: "the fear of all the violence and usurpation that my existing, despite the innocence of its intentions, risks committing." (EN 169)

The third (although there is no sequence here!) moment of

the turn of the face is the opening of humanity, of all the other others and their relations, and of the exigency for justice. It is from this moment that the birth of consciousness and all its possibilities arises.

and finally back to the text: *"From Saying to the Said, or the Wisdom of Desire"*

The first two paragraphs of the selection refer to the scene that I have attempted to set. Signification has its beginnings in the incomparable relation of the same and the absolutely other in proximity. Does this signification survive the assembling of phenomena that is cognition or knowing? Why is such assembling (or scene-setting, for that matter) necessary? Levinas's claim is that "proximity becoming knowing would signify as an enigma" (¶1): the other will show himself in a theme and yet not be reducible to it. The light that proximity changes into will bide its own time, even when it appears to be absorbed in the "high noon without shadows" of being's intelligibility. (133)

The second paragraph states that there would be no problem if proximity ordered to me only the other alone. It would be incorrect to take this as a hypothetical or counterfactual proposition, as if a problem-free life could have been mine *if only* I was left alone with one other person and my immediate responsibility to him. Even with one other person, one must take account of things in order to deal with the problems of keeping peace with him and securing a living for him. Levinas seems to be writing more in the manner of the adage that claims rides for beggars, *if only* wishes were horses. He is, I think, dryly assuring us that there will indeed be nothing but problems - and consequently consciousness - just because proximity does *not* order to me only the other alone. Proximity is always troubled and that trouble is due to the "permanent entry" (¶10) of a third party.

The trouble that the third brings is a complication of relationships. There is a straightforward directness in the immediacy of proximity: "I alone answer, before any question, for my neighbor." (¶3) With the entry of the third there are now human relations that concern me but arise beyond my ken. "The other and the third party, my neighbors, contemporaries of one another, put distance between me and the other and the third party." (ibid.)

The turning of the face of the other and the entry of the third party - in the light of proximity and through the establishment of distance and contemporaneity - induces consciousness and the possibility of my own freedom. To return to the earlier image of the approach of the other as an abrupt awakening and vigilance, this would be the time of accommodation in which your straining eyes and ears begin to discern shapes from the darkness and pick up whispers in the silence. The straining has arisen in response to the other in proximity; the discernment in response to the presence of the neighbor in the light that proximity changes into.[22]

the third party: contradiction and limitation (¶ 3)

The third party introduces a contradiction in the saying whose signification before the other until then went in one direction. It is of itself the limit of responsibility and the birth of the question: What do I have to do with justice? A question of consciousness. (¶ 3)

The birth of consciousness is not the end of the order of proximity. The entry of the third party introduces a contradiction which
will be seen as either an affront to the signification of the one-for-
the-other or to the reason of consciousness. As a substitution, purely
for-the-other, I am exposed in passivity to the other. Saying, before
anything said, bears witness to the other, is the one given over to the
other as a sign. The third party interrupts that, forces me back upon
myself. My presence is required, but my presence distances me from
the other. This distance is the limit of my responsibility. And yet the
other, in the face of my neighbor, in the presence of all the others,
still calls me to my responsibility in a way which does not appear
to consciousness. The origin of this responsibility for my neighbor
has never been present and so cannot be represented or recalled. Its
existence, the existing of this neighbor before me, "is effectuated in
the non-postponable urgency with which he requires a response." (TI
212)

Justice is necessary because I - *qua I*, unique and irreplaceable - am already concerned with peace for "the neighbor *and* the
one far-off" (¶ 3, my emphasis).[23] Justice requires consciousness,
con-scrying, a *knowing*-together: "comparison, coexistence, contemporaneousness, assembling, order, thematization, the visibility of faces,
and thus intentionality and the intellect . . . the intelligibility of a
system, and thence also a copresence on an equal footing as before
a court of justice." (ibid.) Because my infinite responsibility to the
Other is delimited in the presence of the third party, because the face
of the neighbor has become visible, because my presence is required,
because I need to know what has happened, because the third and

the neighbor come to join me in a here and now, because judgment is necessary, because justice is necessary, there is "representation, logos, consciousness, work, the neutral notion *being*." (¶7) The response to the other which began in saying, in the signifyingness of substitution, is "fixed in a said" and bound into "a book, law and science." (ibid.)

We co-exist, you and I and the others, together in a time and place, here and now amongst ourselves and in the world and its history. We may be compared and assembled, thematized, ordered and represented as if we were interchangeable commodities - but "out of representation is produced the order of justice" (¶7), and within its spaces proximity "takes on a new meaning" (¶3). Just because proximity still signifies in consciousness - and "the entry of a third party is the very fact of consciousness" (¶4) - we can judge these necessary acts of judgment, of assembly and comparison, of intellect and intention, and question whether they serve to support or impede us in our responsibility for our neighbors. It is this judgment of judgment in terms of responsibility that limits the violence of justice.

If I am ordered to the absolutely other alone, my responsibility is literally boundless, without boundary, without any thing to be bound by nor destination to be bound for. My response, *me voici,* would never lead to the exposure of a "myself", but would be only a movement of desire, an *I* at the point of departure for the other. Levinas describes this desire, which rests on no prior kinship and does not long for return or anticipate satisfaction, as metaphysical. "It is like goodness - the Desired does not fulfill it, but deepens it. . . . A desire without satisfaction which, precisely, *understands* [*entend*] the remoteness, the alterity, and the exteriority of the other." (TI 34) It is this desire that moves subjectivity in proximity.

In Greek terms, then, the face of my neighbor is *peras* to the *apeiron* of the Other, a limiting principle that gives form to one's illimitable response to the Other. The limit that is presented by the face is a destination or destiny that creates responsibility in the response that was purely Desire. It is productive in the sense that it "forces the issue": the expression of the face calls forth the expression of my responsibility - the possibility and even the duty to give to the other "the bread out of one's own mouth and the coat from one's shoulders." (55) *Il me regarde.* The vulnerability that the neighbor exposes to me is real and it concerns me. My Desire takes form as giving.

The third party provides another sort of limit to responsibility by reference to the relation between the third and the other and my inability to answer completely for the other before the third party. It is a boundary - thus far and no further - to my responsibility and it is this limitation of mine which raises the problem that calls for justice and consciousness. The third party, perhaps outrageously, and without in any way diminishing it, creates a blind spot in my responsibility which calls for judgment. The third and the other present themselves to me as neighbors, each unique and incomparable. At the same time, they come to join me as equals to each other, an original equality which justice assumes. But what has already passed between them is beyond me. If it were just me and my neighbor, my responsibility to him would go so far as to take responsibility for his responsibility, to answer completely for him without reserve. Justice is for the neighbor. His right concerns me before my own. However, so does that of the ones far off: "all the others than the other obsess me." (¶5) In the ethical situation of justice, "the right of the other person - but obtained only after investigation and judgment - is imposed before that of the third." (EN 198) From the moment the third party appears, in "the very name of the absolute obligations toward one's fellow man, a certain abandonment of the absolute allegiance he calls forth is necessary." (EN 203) The contradiction of the immediacy of proximity compels the mediation of consciousness.

the origin of appearing

But still, I have been moving too quickly here. The problem with trying to follow proximity into being is that it's very difficult to actually arrive. "The apparition of a third party is the very origin of appearing, that is, the very origin of an origin." (¶10) Of all the strange things that Levinas has to say, this must be one of the strangest. And everything depends on it. Without precisely and concretely situating the origin of consciousness in the realm of the interhuman and revealing the connection between the interhuman and proximity, all this talk of proximity is merely pleasant chatter, a diversion, a child's fable about goodness.

So, stepping very slowly, what is being said here? "Origin" and "apparition" are two more of the ambivalent terms, like "produce", that mark Levinas's writing. *Origin* is an arising from something, and it is that in which something has its beginning or source or root or cause. It is both a temporal action, a coming-to-be, and the reference site of that action. (In geometry, an origin is a fixed point from which measurement or motion commences, an intersection of axes in Cartesian co-ordinates or a pole in polar co-ordinates.) Similarly, *apparition* is at once the action of appearing, becoming visible, and that which appears, a phenomenon or semblance - or perhaps a spectre, "an immaterial appearance as of a real being" (OED). And so:

- "The apparition of a third party"
  Both the third party making an appearance and his appearance to me
- "is the very origin of appearing"
  is the arising of appearing and the source of its beginning
- "that is,"
  in other words - which indicates an equivalence, or yet more equivocation - the apparition of the third party is
- "the very origin of an origin."

Appearing is an origin, and the apparent beginning of beginnings starts from the spectral arising of the third party before my very eyes. (Whose eyes? *Mine.* Do you see now? *Yes, of course. There you are.*)

It seems that the opening of time and space for the subject must begin from this moment - in the temporality of appearing and the locus of an origin. The opening occurs in the representable bringing-together of me and the one who appears, the one I address as *you.* The apparition of the third party is at once also the birth of consciousness, of a subject that perceives itself with and separate from another, and the origin of dialogue, of a nominative first and second person. The third party, whose thirdness is derived by its participation within the plot of the same and the absolutely other in proximity, manifests *as the second person, as* my neighbor[24], the one who concerns and obsesses me, to whom I am addressed before I address him.

The apparition of the third party is what appears *to me,* is apparent *to me*. Proximity reverts to being and, Levinas writes, "as the 'closer and closer,' becomes the subject . . . Proximity is the subject that approaches and consequently constitutes a relationship in which I participate as a term, but where I am more, or less, than a term." (82) This is a restless subjectivity. As a term in a relationship, the subject is an origin, a starting place for "measurement or motion", but it cannot rest in that term. The self which recurs to itself in its perception and consciousness finds itself already obligated to the other by a responsibility that precedes its own origin. There is a surplus, or lack, "a recurrence which empties me of all consistency." (ibid.)

The signification of subjectivity in proximity is saying and substitution, the subject exposed as a sign given over to the other. Consciousness arises with the appearance of the third party and in my perception of him in relation to me, "closer and closer" - but I am not called to simply take up a position with regard to him, placed over against him. In the relation of proximity in which both the subject and the third party are implicated, the recurrence of the self is "broken up by the difference between terms, in which difference is non-indifference and the break is an obsession." (83) My presence is never safely established in itself. It is always *coram,* in-the-presence-of, always a presence that is called to and for the other. Célan's *"Ich bin du, wenn ich ich bin"* (99) isn't just a poet's flight of fancy. It is an origin, a strange hypostasis.

The apparition or revelation of the third party as neighbor is the other reduced to recourse to me, given over to my responsibility. The third party as an intervention or participation in proximity provides a limit whereby proximity becomes the subject. Earlier, I wondered how the latency of subjectivity became realized, how the hyperbolically passive *I* under accusation gained the agency to *posit itself as I,* to *respond,* and to *find resources.* This is where it happens.

For a very crude analogy, consider an aircraft that approaches the speed of sound. Pressure accumulates in a wave preceding the aircraft and when that wave hits the ground - boom. In proximity, the approach of the Same towards the absolutely Other is infinite, but encounters no resistance. The entry of the third party, the turning of the face, introduces a limit. The approach becomes closer and closer, resistance builds, and then - boom.[25] Proximity becomes the subject and the third party reverts to being, appears as neighbor to the subject, face to face.[26]

This brings us back again to the idea that being ordered to "the other alone" would never be a problem, this time understanding "the other" as the third party/neighbor/second person, the one before me to whom I say "you", the *du* that I am *wenn ich ich bin,* unique and incomparable, beloved. Everything that Levinas has to say about the asymmetry of the relation and my infinite and irrecusable responsibility holds here without question.

Moving slowly ahead, we can see that problems begin with the concomitant and concordant entry or apparition of the third party as a *third person* who, as Levinas describes, is "other than the neighbor, but also another neighbor, and also a neighbor of the other, and not simply his fellow." (¶3) The thirdness of the third party is tied around the approach of the one to the Other. The thirdness of a third person enters the frame of two, my neighbor and myself. At once, I have two neighbors, or even a plenitude, to each of whom I owe everything. There is "me" and "you" and "you". Both of you face me, summon and judge me, look at me "in the eyes of the Other". Justice is required, peace for the nearest as well as for the one far off. (But you my neighbor are always in proximity with me, no matter how physically far off, and the peace that summons me is always the one in which I am implicated and for which I am responsible.)

The third person here is not only another neighbor to me. The third is also the one I can refer to as "he" or "she" in my address to you my neighbor. My allegiance to one may come before my allegiance to the other. But which is which? What has passed between you? Who am I with, and who against?[27] This problem of my responsibility calls for discernment, judgment, consciousness.

> In the comparison of the incomparable there would be the latent birth of representation, logos, consciousness, work, the neutral notion *being*. Everything is together, one can go from the one to the other and from the other to the one, put into relationship, judge, know, ask "what about . . . ?", transform matter. (¶7)

the correction of asymmetry: an other for the others (¶ 6,7)

But what of my right? What of justice for me? Levinas claims that this also arises in relation with the third party. I want to follow this question more closely than Levinas has done. His first concern, rightly, is to elucidate the priority of the responsibility of the "I" to the other, and my right is something that my relationship with my neighbor cannot by any means establish. Signification is absolutely asymmetric. I am for-the-other, subjected to substitution, whereas no one can take the place of my responsibility. There is no condition for this, no ground here upon which I might stake a reciprocal claim for myself - a claim which would, in any event, deny the original goodness of substitution.

A concern for my right does not start from me. It depends upon my being approached "as an other by the others, that is, 'for myself'." (¶ 6). Levinas speaks of this "reverting of the incomparable subject into a member of society" (ibid.) as grace, as a new relation with illeity, as the passing of God. "'Thanks to God' I am another for the others." (ibid.)

"Thanks to God" because to be approached "for myself" is to be approached not for the quiddity of my being, but as absolutely other, incomparable. Just in the same manner as I am originally commanded by illeity and as I approach my neighbor, this is an act of gratuity, disinterested and non-indifferent, a response to what is "otherwise than being". To be approached "for myself" cannot be understood as my due. I am not owed it through an obligation born from, or reducible to, any common identity or debt or desert. Any of these would indeed miss me, mistake the uniqueness and the null-site of my subjectivity. The other, for whom I am a neighbor, approaches me as though responding to an appeal from elsewhere, an appeal that comes from my ungrounded situation of destitution and homelessness, even though it is an appeal which I certainly cannot make for myself without fault, that is, without betraying my own responsibility.

An appeal and a response "thanks to God". Before I am grateful to the one who approaches me as a neighbor, I am "grateful to God", grateful for the goodness that allows me to be approached, for the goodness of an approach that lets me be. It is not that I am an other in the presence of God or that God is "involved as an alleged interlocutor" (¶6). I am an other in the presence of the others, and any relation that binds us, each to the other, binds us in the trace of the passing of God, "in the trace of transcendence, in illeity." (ibid.) Such binding relationships of mutual regard - pledgeable relationships of kinship, enmity, romantic or sympathetic love - do not begin in any economy in which they may find expression. "The passing of God, of whom I can speak only by reference to this aid or this grace, is precisely the reverting of the incomparable subject into a member of society." (ibid.)

Subject to the other as I am, it is the relation with the third party which is "an incessant correction of the asymmetry of proximity in which the face is looked at." (¶6) Why "correction"? Is there something wrong, something mistaken, in this asymmetry? For the *I* in proximity, not at all. Proximity is the relation between the Same and the Other, a relation without relation which does not enclose either term within a unity and which therefore cannot support the possibility of either symmetry or reciprocity. The Other is not present, and yet the Same, latent birth of subjectivity, responds to the Other, more passive than any passivity, without any choice because prior to any freedom. In proximity, I am for-the-other, irreplaceable and incomparable. There is nothing taken and so no possibility of a mis-taking or its correction. There is no possibility at all.

This situation changes - or rather, first becomes situated - in the relation with the third party "in which the face is looked at". Possibility, and the possibility of problems, arises with the consciousness that assembles into being, "and at the same time, in a being, the hour of the suspension of being in possibility . . . the reduction of a being to the possible and the reckoning of possibles, the comparison of incomparables." (¶4)

What is possible once possibility becomes possible? Choice, freedom, capability, beginning, assembling oneself as an ego, revealing the world and its manifestations, taking things up, putting them down, beginning anew, persevering in being. The subject as *conatus* or *cogito*, self-conscious, self-interested, essentially vulnerable from the first to insults and wounding, to persecution and death. The responsibility that goes from the *I* to the Other in proximity can be thematized - as opposed to lived - as an *asymmetric* relation between me and my neighbor only by "the memory that assembles in presence" (¶4), by one to whom the face appears as both visage and the face of faces.

But the origin of this responsibility does not present itself to memory, and indeed is easily forgotten.[28] This other person can be taken as an obstacle or enemy, a competitor for resources, a limit to my freedom. If at the same time I voluntarily recognize some responsibility for him, it will soon strike me as at least unreasonable, if not ridiculous, that such an attitude would be asymmetric, that some form of compensation should not also flow back to me. This, however, is not the problem that Levinas finds in the entry of the third party, a problem of injustice for me that would be "incessantly corrected" in my relationship with the third.

Indeed, the problem for this ego arises elsewhere, from its ambiguous position as both a conscious subject opposed to an object and as belonging to the essence from which it suspends itself. Levinas writes that this "way for the subject to find itself again in essence . . .

is not a harmonious and inoffensive participation." (163) The subject's attempts to subtract itself from essence find no justification, trapping it in "the horrifying *there is* [*il y a*] behind all finality proper to the thematizing ego, which cannot sink into the essence it thematizes." (ibid.)

> But the imperturbable essence, equal and indifferent to all responsibility which it henceforth encompasses, turns, as in insomnia, from this neutrality and equality into monotony, anonymity, insignificance, into an incessant buzzing that nothing can now stop and which absorbs all signification, even that of which this bustling about is a modality. (ibid.)

The absurdity of the *there is,* its insignificance, the overflowing of sense by nonsense, still signifies as a modality of the-one-for-the-other. (164) The appearance of the third party - the "origin of an origin" and "the very fact of consciousness" - makes possible a self-positing ego, indifferent to all responsibility, that can yet maintain itself in the face of its own unjustifiable ascendancy only by ignorance, forgetfulness, or a ruthless will to power. Still, signification can not be assumed. The intellect cannot escape the dank whisperings of the *there is* by taking over for itself the significance of its exclusive subjectivity. It signifies in love, in non-indifference to the other, in disinterest - "the ethical deliverance of the self through substitution for the other . . . an ego awakened from its imperialist dream, its transcendental imperialism, awakened to itself, a patience as a subjection to everything." (ibid.) Awakened to itself in proximity with the other. *Yes?* [29]

The approach of the other in the face of the neighbor calls the subject back to its responsibility, and saves the ego from itself, its "hateful" self (AT 21, citing Pascal), saves it from its own worst excesses paradoxically by calling its very being into question. But, again, being able to represent the relation in consciousness as asymmetric seems to raise a problem for the freedom of the subject.

The asymmetry of its responsibility is not a problem for the self that is for-the-other. The signifyingness of substitution is never assumed or taken on. It is "consumed as an expiation for the other. The self before any initiative, before any beginning, signifies anarchically, before any present." (164) To be a subject is to be subjected to..., to be required to support everything without compensation. "It is in its ex-ception and ex-pulsion as a responsible one that a subject outside of being can be conceived." (163)

For whom, then, can my freedom be a problem? For no one, if not first of all for the one who approaches me as a neighbor. "The relationship with the third party is an incessant correction of the asymmetry of proximity." (¶6) The freedom that concerns me is that of the other person, for him or her I demand every human right. In my uniqueness, as the "chosen one", I have no other course. My rights will have to be, first of all, someone else's business, someone who approaches me as an other, "for myself", in the trace of illeity and also in the presence of all the others, and thereby inaugurates this incomparable subject as a member of society, as one among many.

I am approached as a neighbor, and I am also - just because this approach is also in proximity to other others - included in the census.[30] The relationship with the third party provides a correction as a *counterweight* to asymmetry, incessant because I remain infinitely and always encumbered by my responsibility for and before my neighbor. To be a member of society is to remain first of all responsible for justice for the others - "justice passes by justice in my responsibility for the other" (¶ 5) - but "there is also justice for me." (¶ 7) That this reversion also enables my self-defense still needs to be shown.

the order of justice - and reason (¶ 8,9)

It is perhaps also not yet clear that proximity signifies in one's relationships to others powerfully enough to engender consciousness and to give meaning to reason and "the intelligibility of systems" (¶ 4). I want to turn one last time to the idea that there would be no problems if only I were ordered to "the other alone", this time commencing with the order of the "intimate society" of two. Consider this testimony of a man's experience at the moment of the birth of his first child:

> Unexpectedly and with unprecedented power, my heart felt pierced, my breath left me, and I was sobbing uncontrollably. Tears were washing my face. I felt seized by a superior force. This seizure repeated itself later, when through a window, I was allowed to look at my son who was squirming in the hands of a stranger in the nursery. This time, I had a thought as well as all the unruly emotions: "If anything were to happen to my baby, if he died or even hurt himself, I would die!" The area of the surface of my vulnerability had just doubled. For the first time in my memory, I felt connected, one with

another, for better or worse. I didn't realize then, but that was the moment I ceased to exist as I had been up until then: essentially alone and free. Faced with my son, I immediately became his hostage, and replacing freedom, I was overtaken with responsibility. I felt smitten and shaky. (Feldmár 2000:1)

This is the intimate society of love, of being-for-the-other, of an "I" turned inside out. There is something inordinate about it that risks betrayal even the telling of the experience - and how much more an analysis of that description! Still, one can see how the intimacy of love reduces the world to the lover and the beloved. The only hint of an outside is the dreaded and amorphous "anything" that could happen to harm the child. Anything and everything that is to come enters only into the concern of the father for the son. At the same time, the presence of the baby brings a force to bear on the father that he could never have expected, that he cannot absorb or surmount. This unique particular one was not expected, was not invited, and the father is transformed by the opening of his own defenseless and immediate welcome. This, concretely and absolutely, is the signifying of proximity. To be smitten by "my son" was, from the first, to be smitten by a stranger.

We might also note that this intimate society is in no way a society of equals. Responsibility and being-for goes only in one direction, from the lover to the beloved, and the baby is both less than the father in his physical helplessness and more than him in his capacity to command and overwhelm.

But what happens when this intimacy of two is interrupted by a third who is immediately also a beloved? Perhaps, just to keep the story simple, by the birth of another child who evokes just the same response in the father. Once again he is taken hostage, overwhelmed and responsible in proximity with the shattering alterity of this other - without in any way diminishing his connection with the firstborn. The second child calls into question the innocence of his love for the first with the revelation that this is not an "anything" that has come, but a *someone* who "listens, wounded, to the amorous dialogue, and that with regard to him, the society of love itself is in the wrong." (EN 21) Outside of the control of the lover's intention, the love of one becomes a detriment to this other one. Protests of innocence - "I didn't want that", "I never meant to" - are in vain.

The intimacy of the two has been founded on the devotion of the lover to the beloved: "Love is the *I* satisfied by the *thou*, grasping in the other the justification of its being. The presence of the other exhausts the content of such a society." (EN 20) The arrival of another calls that satisfaction into question, makes of it a fault with regard to the third party. The innocent inequality of love becomes the fault of privilege: "a special grant of immunity or advantage", the word itself derived from *privare* + *lex,* already a separation from the law.[31] This fault which has arisen outside the grasp of an intentional consciousness, this hyperextension of what one is answerable for, is the very mode of "thirdness" in Levinas's usage.

As the responsible *I*, obsessed by this one and this one, the father must look from the one to the other, must compare, must inquire, and know, and judge. With the entry of the third party, another other, the *I* is in proximity with a human plurality which limits responsibility and moderates or measures the substitution of the one for the other (¶3,7). "[A]ll the excess of generosity that I must have toward the other is subordinated to a question of justice." (AT 102) Love makes way for justice.

There is thus a paradoxical betrayal in this first act of intentional consciousness: the alterity of the face is renounced in order to consider its situation, to ask, to compare, to bring together the heteronomous parts of this human plurality into a totality or a system - an act which itself founds the justice called for by one's very obligation to the face which remains exterior to any system.

With the arrival of the third person, the self finds itself even further accused. Not only is my presence in the world - the "Da" of Da-sein - unjustified with regard to the other who I may have displaced, now I am accountable for faults that are incurred beyond what I could intend, faults that now occur in a society. "But if fault is now outside the realm of what can be assessed by an examination of conscience, man as an interiority loses all importance . . . The subject at fault awaits the meaning of his being from outside; he is no longer the man confessing his sins, but the one acquiescing to accusations." (EN 23) That one's conscience is not enclosed in oneself, that its voice does not begin from me, bears witness again to subjectivity as a relation with transcendence, as being-for-the-other. In the presence of the third party, the self is expiation insofar as it can, as ego, conjugate identity and alterity without violence.

As a social being whose consciousness in this sense resides outside of itself, I am profoundly connected to all the others, to these faces that look to me even if I never look directly at them.[32] My singularity is a function of this responsibility before them, and it is language that enables my link with this exteriority to be without violence. "*An exteriority without violence is the exteriority of discourse.*" (EN 22)

> It is practiced between beings, between substances who do not enter into their words, but who proffer them. The transcendence of the interlocutor and the access to the other through language show that man is a singularity - a singularity other than that of the individuals who are subsumed under a concept or who articulate moments of it. The *I* is ineffable because it is speaking par excellence; respondent, responsible. The other as pure interlocutor is not a known, qualified content, apprehensible on the basis of some general idea, and subject to that idea. He faces things, in reference only to himself. Only with speech between singular beings is the interindividual meaning of beings and things, that is, universality, constituted. (EN 26)

To go from one to another, to ask "what about..." is to ask *someone*, to appeal, to open a discourse. Consciousness begins in the exposure of my insufficiency and need. My responsibility, which has become a problem, calls for con-sciousness, for knowing together, for the manifestation of reason in discourse. The assembly that justice requires is not simply a bringing together of objects to reveal their essential truths, but an association, an opening to sociality. *Saying* must go beyond its straightforward exposure to say something said to someone, to present oneself in the presence of another. In this co-presence, situations must be represented and understood, tested and witnessed, totalized and investigated, theorized and abstracted.

To return again to the text under discussion: "The saying is fixed in a said, is written, becomes a book, law and science." (¶7)

For Levinas, "[o]ut of representation is produced the order of justice" (ibid.), but the work of justice is not an impersonal or objective representation. "My relationship with the other as neighbor gives meaning to my relations with all the others." (¶8) "The other as neighbor" is the one to whom and for whom I am already responsible, the other who turns to face me, vulnerable in his own skin, and at the same time, the one who bears within his flesh the trace of an infinite alterity, an alterity to which my responsibility bears witness. Proximity signifies in subjectivity as the-one-for-the-other. But in the relationship with the others who are already "reduced to recourse to me", proximity takes a step back or is further reduced by the complication of responsibility that ensues. It still signifies in representation to the extent that the intimacy of love is limited by the exigency for justice and the distance of difference is limited by the communion of non-indifference.

Justice is not a concept: it is a work which is enacted within the social realm of being and beings.[33] The subjectivity of the *I* is first founded in substitution, in an exposure to the Other in proximity which fails to ensure a place of its own, but society itself is then founded by this very subjectivity for whom responsibility has become a problem. The self forms "the unity of human society, which is one in my responsibility." (197, n. 22) This unity is a partial - in both senses - reduction by the self of the heterogeneity of the others to a totality in which judgments and discernments are made in order that the work of justice can be done. Partial because I and the others can disengage from the totality, and partial because the assembly is made in service of the others. "The self is a *sub-jectum*; it is under the weight of the universe, responsible for everything. The unity of the universe is not what my gaze embraces in its unity of apperception, but what is incumbent on me from all sides, regards me in the two senses of the word, accuses me, is my affair." (116)

As in the poem of my epigraph, I am *the center of the universe* - but to be the center of the universe is not to be its master. Durcan hides this confession in the delicacy of a comma, a hesitation before the conditional in the refrain: "*I'm always here, if you want me.*" At the center of the center of the universe is an openness to and for the other.

Of course, to find oneself the center of the universe never precludes anyone else from doing so as well. This does not imply the relativism of a multitude of private universes occupying separate or-bits. One's universe always goes so far as to include also the neighbor's responsibility.

> The interhuman, properly speaking, lies in a non-indifference of one to another, in a responsibility of one for another, but before the reciprocity of this responsibility, which will be inscribed in impersonal laws, comes to be superimposed on the pure altruism of this responsibility inscribed in the ethical position of the *I qua I*. (EN 100)

Indeed, it is the presence of other responsible ones which opens the interhuman order of respect - different from the intimate order of love - which "attaches the just man to his associates in justice before attaching him to the man who demands justice . . . a relationship between equals." (EN 35) The inequality of the intimate society of love or proximity becomes the equality of respect in a *true society:* "a configuration of wills which concern each other through their works, but who look one another in the face" (EN 20).

works of justice (¶8,9,15)

> We are we because, commanding from identity to identity, we are disengaged from the totality and from history. But we are *we* in that we command each other to a work through which we recognize each other. To be disengaged from the totality while at the same time accomplishing a work in it is not to stand against the totality, but for it - that is, in its service. To serve the totality is to fight for justice. The totality is constituted by violence and corruption. The work consists in introducing equality into a world turned over to the interplay and the mortal strife of freedoms. (EN 36)

Levinas presents us with a certain configuration of relationships - of I, the Other, my neighbor, all the others - all of which bear the trace of the Infinite. Each is an immediate and passive experience of the *I,* constituting its subjectivity as unique and situating its identity as both a term of the relationship with the other and its modality. Here I am. Each relationship signifies in proximity as substitution, as the-one-for-the-other. Each begins from an original, pre-historic and anarchic responsibility to and for the other, which leads the *I* into difficulty when face-to-face with a host of others. Hence the need for justice, for consciousness, which means assembly in a common time and place, representation.

The *I* takes on the role of a thinking subject just because this assembling is not a sure thing. It involves placing some quantity of available elements together within an available system and is always susceptible to "chances or delays, and something like good or bad luck . . . subjectivity in retention, memory and history, intervenes to hasten the assembling, to confer more chances for the packing in, to unite the elements into a present, to re-present them." (133-4) Through such conception, "intuition ceases to be blind." (ibid.)

Substitution in proximity is an original goodness. In the presence of the others for whom justice is necessary, the *I* reverts to a self occupied with consciousness through the limitation of the infinite responsibility of proximity. Goodness, in the work of justice that lends it vision, now becomes a possibility that is available to the subject within the realm of the interhuman. Levinas calls this goodness *holiness*, an absolute ideal which "may define the anthropological over and beyond its genus" (59) - "the human possibility of giving the other priority over oneself." (EN 109)

Levinas writes that the work of justice "consists in introducing equality into a world turned over to the interplay and the mortal strife of freedoms." (EN 36) There are two notions to be understood here: the introduction of equality, and a "world turned over". Equality itself must be seen as arising first in the turn from the proximity of the Other to the appearance of the face. The first equality in the world is the equality - an equality of infinities - of my responsibility to this one and to all the others. If this were not so, there would be no problem, no question of justice, no need for consciousness. The other, the stranger, presents himself to me as an equal by reference to the third party. (TI 213) The "other is from the first the brother of all the other men" (¶5), they are each other's contemporaries. If, after investigation and judgment, the right of the other person is then imposed before that of the third, this still refers to an initial equality - an equality that is not derived from any essential likeness or commonality between them, but because my relationship with my neighbor "gives meaning to my relations with all the others" (¶8). My relationship with my neighbor *qua* neighbor is a relation with transcendence, with a radical exteriority, with alterity. Awakening for the Other *(yes?)*, I find myself face-to-face with my neighbor. Alterity manifests as difference - the Other becoming others without diminishment or degradation - and this difference with regard to me signifies as non-indifference, calls for justice, for the introduction into the world of an equality of all that is borne by my inequality, without compensation, in a passivity prior to judgment or freedom. "All human relations as human proceed from disinterestedness." (¶8)

Justice is "the necessary interruption of the Infinite being fixed in structures, community and totality." (¶11) But - like the subject, like the Face - justice is another breaking and binding place, another gateway, a hyphen, an aporia. It is at once the fixing of the Infinite and the "entry of the diachrony of proximity . . . into the synchrony of the said" (ibid.). It is due to this ambiguity that justice "is impossible without the one that renders it finding himself in proximity." (¶8) Citing Plato's *Gorgias* (190, n. 35; 199, n. 25), Levinas takes note that in the absolute judgment of the other - a direct relationship - both the judge and the judged are stripped of every quality that would absorb proximity and establish a community between them: "the dead judge the dead".

But there is also found "the necessity of a 'certain community' in justice between the judge and the judged . . . a European who judges the Europeans, and . . . an Asiatic who judges the Asiatics." (ibid.) The one who renders justice finds himself as well in the order of being, in community in the world. This qualified judgment requires that the judge be a peer of the judged, able to appreciate his or her situation and circumstances also in terms of their commonality or equality in a world that Levinas characterizes as "turned over to the interplay and mortal strifes of freedoms."

The possibility of justice in the world opens as well the possibility of error and the possibility of injustice, "the possibility of not awakening to the other; there is the possibility of evil. Evil is the order of being pure and simple." (EN 114)[34]

Justice, as the necessary interruption of the Infinite, is a risky business. The *I* reduced to ego and installed as a member of society, the incomparable others assembled together in comparison, the associates with whom I join in the work, the social structures that are set up: all of these take place in the world and are "at every moment on the point of having their center of gravitation in themselves, and weighing on their own account." (¶8) It is possible that being will take itself too seriously, more seriously than it can bear.

By comparison with the "extreme gravity" of responsibility in proximity, Levinas writes, "being appears like a game. Being is play or detente, without responsibility, where everything possible is permitted." (6) It is a play of interest, a game always with something at stake even up to "an interplay and strife of mortal freedoms". Without that comparison with responsibility, human being expresses itself for itself, an expression of free will, of power and perseverance, opposed to other wills, to nothingness or to death. The world is an arena of competition for a multitude of freedoms and interests. The self goes out from and returns to itself: self-identical, self-conscious, self-interested. The others are conceived as "them", a mass of alter egos, to be befriended or feared, ignored or made use of. My neighbors and I congeal into an "us", not joined together for justice, "command[ing] each other to a work through which we recognize each other", but as if founded by our shared identity, culture, or common interest. The state and its structures are founded as tools of "social equilibrium... harmonizing antagonistic forces." (¶8)

It is as though human being signified only in its existence, as if perseverance or persistence in being could be taken as its own beginning and justification. Not only is everything possible permissible, but everything possible can be claimed and taken over as a right by those with the power and will to do so. In a world turned over to the "interplay and the mortal strifes of freedoms", one that has forgotten the "extreme gravity" of responsibility, it becomes easily apparent - at least to the mighty - that might indeed equals right.

But can it be taken for granted that righteousness is a force that being can fully assume or take credit for? The exigency for justice, before or beyond any doing of mine, is first of all the appeal of the exploited one, the disenfranchised one, the refugee. Those who are excluded within the totality, or without it. Justice signifies as the entry of the radically other into a system that cannot contain it, like the thought of infinity exceeds the mind that thinks it. Justice signifies as the "entry of the diachrony of proximity . . . into the synchrony of the said". It is not that the Law (the Said), resting in itself, expands its reach to the "previously disadvantaged", bringing everyone together under its rule. Rather, it is through injustice that "'all the foundations of the earth are shaken'" (45). The appeal from the face of the other puts the Law in question, puts the State in question, puts "us" in question, puts "me" in question. What have I to do with justice? The force of the appeal, and hence the exigency for justice, cannot be reduced to interest and essence. If it can reach me it is because I find myself already implicated: if it can reach me I have already acknowledged my fault, my responsibility, my relation with the other in proximity that precedes and conditions consciousness or memory, that precedes my relation with myself. In the passivity of substitution for the other, in the patience of sensibility and remorse, "the distinction between being accused and accusing oneself" is "effaced" (125).

To be put in question, to be accused, is to be turned again to the pre-origin of being, the originary transcendent relationship with the other, to return from the said to the saying, the *I* exposed to the other, exposing its exposure, giving itself as a sign. "The forgetting of self moves justice." (¶ 9) And, at once, it is to be turned back to oneself "by the extraordinary commitment of the other to the third party" (¶ 13), to engage in discourse, to search for justice, to introduce equality, to establish communities and structures in which the work of justice may be done. In this necessary interruption of the Infinite, the self-conscious self again is vulnerable to the allure of its own vitality and the threat of death and risks forgetting the goodness that signifies under the seemingly mechanical and anonymous workings of biological and rational necessity.

Conception and intervention, arising from responsibility, are acts of justice. At the same time, as a reduction of proximity to being, of alterity to similarity and difference, they are acts of corruption and violence. The world conceived of is alternately the "original locus of justice" (¶11) - a refuge for the self and a common terrain shared with the others - and a world "turned over to the interplay and the mortal strife of freedoms." The fulcrum of this ambivalence is the egoic self still obsessed by the other and unable to rest in itself. And behind or beneath its motion, turning and returning, appearing and effacing, passes infinity or the transcendent which

> does not let itself be assembled. Removing itself from every memorable present, a past that was never present, it leaves a trace of its impossible incarnation and its inordinateness in my proximity with the neighbor, where I state, in the autonomy of the voice of conscience, a responsibility, which could not have begun in me, for freedom, which is not my freedom. (¶15)

philosophy's reason

The work of justice entails service to both the other and to the totality. It is because the self is already in proximity, already for-the-other (already earlier than it could be for-itself or its own death) that one is able to disengage from the totality in order to accomplish works - of consciousness, of justice - within it, and so it is the relationship of proximity that makes them comprehensible. "This means that nothing is outside of the control of the responsibility of the one for the other. It is important to recover all these forms beginning with proximity" (¶8). To comprehend or recover these works, these forms, is the task of philosophy.

"Responsibility for the others or communication is the adventure that bears all the discourse of science and philosophy. Thus
this responsibility would be the very rationality of reason or its universality, a rationality of peace." (¶9) Philosophy is a con-vers-ation.[35]
This sense of a restless and relentless turning together is everywhere
in Levinas's work. Everything moves. Every thing moves in desire, in
relationship with being's other, a transcendent "otherwise than being".
The unique and chosen *I* that reverts into myself, the Face with which
the other breaks through to me and *I* as the neighbor who suffers and
commands my response, the exigent and ambivalent order of justice:
these are the gateways or the expressions of that uncanny relating,
enigmatically borne witness to in responsibility.

Levinas writes, "Philosophy is called upon to conceive ambivalence, to conceive it in several times." (¶15) Philosophy is *called upon,*
invoked and commanded, because justice is necessary. The problem of
responsibility - which is the problem of the suffering of my neighbors,
near and far-off - gives rise to the need for comparison, judgment,
and discrimination, for reason and its principles. Philosophy is called
upon *to conceive* - to bear, to bear in mind, to take in and to hold
- *ambivalence:* "contrary or parallel meanings or the simultaneous
existence of conflicting desires." Beneath or behind all of its projects
and accomplishments, philosophy turns in desire: philosophy yearns.

Stuck firmly on this side of being, the discourse of philosophy
is like a finger pointing to the moon of an exteriority which resists
reduction and evades the grasp of any *logos.* And yet, philosophy is
called upon to take the measure of Infinity, to thematize the unthematizable, to synchronize the diachrony of proximity, to convey the

ineffable even "at the price of a betrayal which philosophy is called upon to reduce." (¶15) It is no wonder that skepticism is philosophy's constant shadow. But this is not at all a finding of philosophy's futility. Philosophy is a conversation between us about the world and each other. Discourse, as a non-violent relation between one another, retains the possibility - however rarely realized or sustained - of peace in a community of works and wills, bound by the freedom of its parts, in which we also "look one another in the face", in which proximity is not absorbed.

The syncopated recurrences of truth and skepticism are not the despair of philosophy but the "glory of illeity" which "overflows both cognition and the enigma through which the Infinite leaves a trace in cognition" (¶15). To conceive ambivalence *in several times* means to bear in mind that the apparent simultaneity of ambivalence is a construction of consciousness, and that this simultaneity does not mean precisely "at the *same* time". It means to bear the separateness of the time of the other. The relationship with illeity to which my responsibility for and before my neighbor testifies does not belong to the temporality of knowing, of essence, of identity and change. It is present to the self only as a trace of what has never arrived or is yet to come, an absent condition of being. The Infinite "comes to pass" in the immediacy of sensibility, contact, and substitution, an immediacy without beginning or end, a diachronic *now* of the one-for-the-other which appears to temporal and reflective consciousness as ambivalence, enigma or paradox. The recovery of these contretemps starting with proximity is the task of philosophy, thus called upon

to conceive ambivalence, to conceive it in several times. Even if it is called to thought by justice, it still synchronizes in the said the diachrony of the difference between the one and the other . . . as non-indifference to the other. Philosophy is the wisdom of love at the service of love. (¶15)

Chapter III. The Orders of Violence

This study began with Levinas's question of how a struggle against violence - which is not necessarily a refusal of violence - could avoid instituting further violence. The question itself implies that there must be a difference between violences. This implication is repeated in the paradox of justified violence which distinguishes between an aggressive violence which fights to conquer and a just (and justifiable) violence which responds in resistance to aggression.

The limitations of justification have been described and developed in the theory of just war in terms of just cause, just conduct, and just ends. The initiative, the force, and the consequences of aggression are seen to provide the rationale and the measure for justifiable violent resistance in the form of retaliation or retribution. Justifiability is called for in the name of aggression's victim, but remains bound by law and by reason. The sanction against violence is maintained in its conditional suspension: justification - making righteous - could only be required for wrongful acts. Justification, as a judgment, is retrospective to the act of resistance or anticipates retrospection within it.

It doesn't seem that this sort of understanding of justification is good enough. In the first place, if justifiability is by some means quantifiable, if it could be adequately accounted for by law or practical reason, it should as a matter of course absolve the possibility of bad conscience or regret for the one who has justifiably retaliated. Such a quantification seems practicably unlikely and, to the extent that such absolution could be taken as license, this unlikelihood is not a bad thing at all. Secondly, the original sanction against violence is not clarified, and neither is the sense that effective non-violent resistance is better than a resistance that makes use of its full allocation of force.

Finally, justification as judgment and as making-right appears to be more concerned with measuring equity and equilibrium than it is with a more profound sense of human justice. It fails to account for the gut sense that resistance to aggression is, in the act, *doing-right*, action that is called-for, obliged, bound not so much by natural law or reason, but by something like justice, something like righteousness - even if the violence of this resistance then still needs to be accounted for and justified in the former sense. This ambivalence of justification exposed in turn an ambivalence in the concept of resistance which indicated a still earlier enigma at the heart of subjectivity.

The second part of this study then turned to the work of Emmanuel Levinas in order to provide a theoretical base for a deeper investigation of the significance of this dilemma. There are several key concepts: proximity and diachrony and the "hither side of" or "otherwise than" being; subjectivity as being-for-the-other, or substitution; the approach and presentation of the other by the face; and consciousness as arising in the subject through an exigency for justice in the presence of all the others.

My review of Levinas's description of the role of the third party in the birth of consciousness ended with his remarks that philosophy is called "to conceive ambivalence in several times" and that it is important to "recover all these forms beginning with proximity", that is, as within "the control of the responsibility of the one for the other." (159) In *Totality and Infinity*, Levinas writes: "Like a shunt every social relation leads back to the presentation of the other to the same without the intermediary of any image or sign, solely by the expression of the face." (TI 213)

The task of this chapter then will be to follow justification and its kin back to the source, back to the presentation of the other and the responsibility of the same, to conceive violence and resistance as interhuman relationships beginning with proximity.

what's the problem?

Levinas says that the true problem is not to refuse violence. Not so much. Why not? What's wrong with making a principled commitment to renounce violence entirely? Very simply: non-violence as a commitment or principle can fail both justice and its own integrity, if it begs the question of justice.

As I have suggested, a tactic of non-violence may not be effective enough against an aggressor. Bad guys fight to win. In the presence of a brutal and intransigent enemy, a pre-emptive and comprehensive refusal of violent resistance may prolong the suffering of aggression. It could effectively be collaboration. That's not good enough. Similarly, my refusal to take up arms might mean that I am reneging on my responsibility, that my refusal is, in fact, not *non-violence* but *non-resistance* - as Levinas writes, a "blanching in non-resistance to evil".

It is also difficult to ensure that violence is comprehensively refused in resistance. Consider acts of civil disobedience or defiance. They may be non-violent in their execution but at the same time they demonstrate a potential force, a violence under rein. Non-violent resistance is not good enough if it is not effective, or if it provokes further aggression. But even in the event that merely the threat of retaliatory force proves effective, it is still coercion and still dependent on the might of the resistance. As a tactic this is fine, certainly better than the use of force, but if it is supposed to spring from a principled refusal of violence, it is somewhat unconvincing. A similar situation holds where judicial systems of corporal punishment are set up as deterrents to violent crime. To put it another way, a simple refusal of violence is not good enough because, to use Levinas's language, it does not recognize that resistance is *already* bound by illeity, in the midst of proximity, already pledged to peace with both "the neighbor and the one far off", already responsible for all of the other others.

If the true problem is not (so much) to refuse violence, one could perhaps distinguish different sorts of violences, one sort - aggressive - to be refused, and another - defensive or just - which may be called upon against another's aggression. Is defensive violence good enough in a struggle against violence? Levinas says not, inasmuch as it itself institutes and legitimates violence. Even as a lack of resistance encourages violence, retaliation engenders it.[36]

If we are to imagine a struggle against violence that is good enough, it will not begin with a simple renunciation of violence, and it will not end with the justification or rationalization of forceful resistance. Good enough would be justice, and justice goes back to the responsibility of the one for all of the others. The "good enough" of a struggle against violence has to be an expression in the world of the original goodness of the approach and welcome of the Other in proximity.

The problem is not so much to refuse violence as to remember that such a refusal hearkens back to the original anarchic appeal of the Other by which I am uniquely elected to responsibility, and through which the neighbor presents himself along with all the others who concern me. Justice is necessary, which means the ordering of inordinate responsibilities, the comparison of incomparables, consciousness, and representation. Peace is incumbent upon me.

A struggle against violence that would be good enough must recognize that resistance to aggression begins not as self-defense but as a spontaneous response to - and responsibility for - the injustice done a neighbor. The doing-right that justifies resistance comes from this implication of oneself in the suffering of another. *Justification is not a declaration of self-righteousness, but a confession of responsibility by a self accused before the face of a neighbor.* The desire for effective nonviolent resistance - which is, after all, the reluctance to do violence even to an aggressor - is also not just the result of a self-interested calculation of consequences or fear of insufficient grounds for rationalization but arises from a fear of one's responsibility for the death of an enemy. In this sense, the enemy also looks at me with the face of a neighbor. The paradox of just war arises precisely in the consciousness of these antagonistic and irremissible responsibilities.

the anarchic ancestry of resistance and aggression: "good violence"

The awakening of the Same to the Other in proximity, at the cusp of a dawn, is the anarchical prototype - the an-archetype, if you will - of resistance. *Here I am,* a presence expressed, a position apposite to the approach of the Other. Here I am where I am found. A resistance, like a silent beacon at the end of a horizonless sea, standing alone in opposition to the infinity traversed by the Other. Resistance, earlier than being, of a potency breaking free of the monotony of the *there is*. A resistance that arcs across the interval which joins and separates Same and Other, that interval which is always augmenting, and always closer than a hair's breadth. Resistance as a component of Desire, earlier than eros. The offering of presence.

And yet, of course, not an offering and not a presence. Prior to consciousness, choice, or intention, resistance as a mode of proximity is pure saying, an offering that is purely passive - because unable to take itself up in time in order to offer itself - of a presence without extension, pure position like a geometric point, oriented only to the Other, saying itself only in response to the Other, a singular term of a unique relation. *Me voici.*

In the same manner, the approach of the Other in proximity is somehow the an-archetype of aggression, moving out and into the resistance of the *I*, the latency of the self. Not just coming to meet, but provoking, invoking and invading, inscribing itself at the innermost beginning of the Same. But if the approach is the pre-historic ancestor of aggression, the significance of its violence must still be considered.

I have already noted a distinction between the "bad violence" of aggression and the "just violence" of resistance to aggression. In the approach of the Other, Levinas finds, remarkably, a "good violence":

The responsibility for another is precisely a saying prior to anything said. The surprising saying which is a responsibility for another is against the "winds and tides" of being, is an interruption of essence, a disinterestedness imposed with a good violence. (43)

The violence here is an imposition, "an interruption of essence", but - to carry on with my conceit that after Levinas one might speak as if proceeding from proximity - what is there in *me voici* to be violated? There is as yet no subject, no will, no freedom, no consciousness, no sentience. No time, no common ground.

The violences of war and being require simultaneity. Aggression comes to claim the place of the victim and resistance arises to take it back. There is engagement, here and now, for the fate of the here and now, in the shared terrain of the living. Proximity, however, is diachronic. There is an irreducible difference between terms. The Other does not come empirically, does not take place at all. In Levinas's precise phrase, the Infinite only "comes to pass". The Infinite cannot touch me, and yet I am touched. The Other does not move me, and yet I am moved. Prior to the emergence of consciousness, what is there that could be charged by the Other, could be entered, other than the strange resistance of the *I*, this offering of presence by the one who is incapable of either?[37] The violence of the Other imposes upon an involuntary openness. This imposition is goodness.

The imposition is election, my election as the unique responsible one, in which I am assigned without any possibility of slipping away. In extreme passivity, on "the hither side" of freedom/non-freedom, choice/coercion, activity/passivity, I am exposed in exposedness to the Other. The strange permeable resistance that the approach finds, that untimely promise of presence, takes place in the approach as a substitution for the other, is "filled up" - or even overfilled, overwhelmed and unable to gather in the other - becomes animated, inspired, obsessed. Becomes, in a return, ego.[38]

The propriety of proximity, this combination of resistance and approach, approach and withdrawal, passivity and assignation, election prior to identity and responsibility prior to freedom, *lets me be.* But one must immediately insist that this subject is not yet in time, but "is diachrony itself" (57). The ego unites identity and alterity: it is the expiation for the violence of the choice (118). Still prior to intention, the expiation itself is not a choice or an exertion of being. It is goodness, a goodness despite oneself. The imposition "invests me in my obedience to the hidden Good" (ibid.). It is the exteriority of alterity and the goodness of goodness that is able to counterbalance and redeem the outrageous forcefulness of the approach of the Other.[39] The good violence in proximity, this order to the other, is the an-archetype - prior to any morality - of the situation of ethics.

The first arrival, so to speak, of "good violence" is this step the Other takes into the porous resistance of a latent subjectivity, the calling forth, evocation or invocation, of a *me voici.* The second is the appearance of the third party or the visible face of my neighbor. Proximity becomes the subject and the other reverts to being, appears as neighbor to the subject, face to face. If the approach could be thought of - however ridiculously - as an outside inducing an emptiness to responsibility, this appearance is of that which orders the response to itself. Breaking into being,[40] into visibility, and yet bearing the trace of illeity, the face presents itself before me, presents itself to me as my concern, regards me, subjects me to my sovereignty as the responsible one. And, at once, all the other others present their equal claims to me, demanding justice, and hounding me into consciousness, commanding me to consider them, to take their measure. As proximity becomes being, as the terms of all these relations come into view, the force and resistance which prevails between them, the attraction and repulsion, "breaking and binding", continues to signify this diachronic or transcendent anarchic beginning in proximity and responsibility for the other.

The first two instances of good violence involve the approach of the Other and the hypostasis of the subject, proximity giving way to being. The third order of good violence appears from the other direction. It is the interruption of being by its other, the violence of the Face that accomplishes the rupture of a conscious subject caught up in itself and its enjoyment of the world.[41] This violence is again expiated by illeity, the trace or the withdrawal of the Other which leaves me to my freedom, and the archaic openness or passivity or goodness of responsibility, of the one-for-the-other. There is more evidently a violation in this contravention of consciousness and enjoyment, but the resistance that is provoked in me finds no aggressor but itself at fault, finds itself already responsible before the neighbor. And yet, in the return of finding oneself responsible, the intrusion by the face continues and deepens, as in a persecution:

> The more I return to myself, the more I divest myself, under the traumatic effect of persecution, of my freedom as a constituted, willful, imperialist subject, the more I discover myself

to be responsible; the more just I am, the more guilty I am. I am "in myself" through the others. The psyche is the other in the same, without alienating the same. (112)

"Good violence" has the effect of moving the subject from latent proximity with the other to the instantiation of the ego and then delivers the self from imperialist self-aggrandizement to expiation and atonement by means of the relentless and unjustifiable accusation and obsession that is the neighbor's face. It is, of course, this last step which must confound reason. The irrevocable claim of the other upon the self is not staked on any empirical ground. It is not enforceable on its own terms, and it is certainly not enforceable purely on being's terms. Good violence, so called, is characterized both by this forcefulness which brooks no defense and by the reticence or impotence of proximity. Like Zeno's arrow, its aim is true even as its impact is infinitely delayed. And yet, this blow affects (even effects) me. There appears a resultant where there has been no opposition. And thereafter the self can find no rest in itself, from either the rational unjustifiability of its own separation from essence or the urgent appeal and command of the face of the neighbor.

It is incorrect to think that the approach of the other is violent just because I am without a choice. This violence has nothing to do with my will. Will is irrelevant here. The approach is violent because I cannot absorb it. It is violent because it comes from outside of my time and space. I cannot conceive of it. I can't catch up with it. I cannot say a word. To be with the other in proximity is to be outside of logos, *apo-logos*. There is only pure saying there, mute and ineffectual apology, the subject expressing itself, expressing expressing, giving itself over as a sign. This is the absolute beginning of signifying.

We can recognize that in proximity we are in the realm of violence because we are outside the reach of language. One could suggest that the lack of words, the lack of testimony, indicates only that nothing has happened. But isn't that exactly how the disaster takes place? To be lost for words indicates violence, catastrophe, being dis-associated, being struck dumb. The other comes to me from I-don't-know-where, out of the blue, unbidden, unexpected, undesired. This "wherever", as far as I can tell, is the same place from which my death or any violence will come to me (TI 233).[42] There is no way to differentiate the nocturnal traumas of death and the other. Only after the event, only after one "finds one's voice", does it become possible to represent the approach - although only in the language of nonsense or betrayal.

In *The Writing of the Disaster*, Maurice Blanchot writes: "The disaster does not put me into question, but annuls the question, makes it disappear - as if along with the question, "I" too disappeared in the disaster which never appears." (Blanchot 1995:28) In the disaster which is the turning of the face, this "disappearance" is the most passive passivity of the ego in which the other is welcomed. It is *substitution*. The ego reverts to its self behither its identity, turned inside out between activity and passivity, torn up from its place by the other, violated, persecuted, reduced to pure expression, a wordless apology.

The violence of the face is also, at the same time, a liberation for me. "[T]he proximity of the neighbor in its trauma does not only strike up against me, but exalts and elevates me, and, in the literal sense of the term, inspires me." (124) Here is the goodness of this "good violence". Suffering by the other becomes suffering *for* the other (125). The subject is set up as a unique and irreplaceable one in responsibility. The approach that traumatizes me also lets me be me. It saves me from myself, saves me for myself, for the other.

But this result is not *why* it is good. The Good, being above or otherwise than essence, is not relative nor instrumental. The Good is good "*in itself* and not by relation to the need to which it is wanting" (TI 103):

> In reality what is at issue is an order where the very notion of the Good first takes on meaning; what is at issue is society. Here the relation connects not terms that complete one another and consequently are reciprocally lacking to one another, but terms that suffice to themselves. This relation is Desire, the life of beings that have arrived at self-possession. (ibid.)

From the forced silence of a trauma or an annihilation - *ex nihilo* - is created the self, a "*signification without a context*" (TI 23), the *I* elected in the approach. *Me voici,* exposed to the other and beckoning the other, prior to any intention or image in a relation that ruptures any theme that could account for it. With the turning of the neighbor's face and the appearance of the others, I come to myself: *Here I am.*

And so we come round again to the whole adventure of being and the particular possibility of speech, discourse, and peace, where communication is a witnessing of infinity, and to speak is first of all to reveal one's own vulnerability to the other. It will be a restless peace, but this return to logos in responsibility is the way by which these "terms that suffice to themselves" can be in relation with each other without either crushing or being crushed by the other.

Here is also the violence of goodness, just because this non-violence is guaranteed only so long as I am held hostage, continually under the persecution of the approach, only so long as the self is an expiation for this persecution that it undergoes, that overwhelms it. To return to Blanchot:

> Responsibility is innocent guilt, the blow always long since received which makes me all the more sensitive to all blows. It is the trauma of creation or of birth. If the creature is "he whose situation is ceded to him by the other", then I am created responsible. My responsibility is anterior to my birth just as it is exterior to my consent, to my liberty. I am born thanks to a favor which turns out to be a predestination - born unto the grief of the other, which is the grief of all. (Blanchot 1995:22)

"Good violence" is the violence of creation. Subjectivity is set upon by the other, bears the other like maternity, in a self that is a relation, the one-for-the-other. In the order of proximity, this unique relation is maintained as an unavoidable, unassumable, and non-reciprocal responsibility and substitution of the self for the other. In the order of sociality, it is maintained as speech, the expression of the one to the other and the other to the one. To maintain the relation means to retain both a separation and a bond between the terms. The separation is achieved in proximity by the alterity of the other and the position of the one, the resistance or presence it submits. The transcending bond is in the approach and the welcome of the other, something like desire. However, this relation becomes exposed in the order of being. As an ego, I am empirically separate from the other, distinct in both body and consciousness, and this distinction gives force to a new self-protective resistance. For intentional consciousness, which is consciousness of . . ., the bond and the separation of being for-the-other is rather an obsession or persecution, a perverse desire for the undesirable. One is besieged, actuated from elsewhere, hunted down in one's own lair. It is a trauma, disaster, the breakup of time, the suppression of distance, the "denucleation" of one's self.

bad violence

If a violence that causes the fission of one's very identity is understood to be a *good* violence, what could be the evil of aggressive violence? Levinas claims that every social relation leads "like a shunt" back to proximity and the expression of the face. If so, the evil of violence must be sought back that far. A brief description of the phenomenality of aggression will aid us in this pursuit.

There are three situations in which one can experience aggression: as an aggressor against another, as the target of another's aggression, and as a witness of an aggression between others. In all of these, aggressivity is produced within the common time and place of consciousness and being where each one is sovereign in his or her own place. Aggression aims to expand that agency, to take an inner experience of identity and perpetuate it, to universalize the forcefulness of being in the world.

As an aggressor, my identity corresponds with my will and my power and that will and power, that *jouissance*, is constrained in its drive for expression and expansion by the presence of the others, by their enjoyments and expropriations within a shared field of resources. In competition for these resources (or pre-emptively, in order that they fall under my control), the power of identity assumes the force of aggression. My aggression serves to enlarge me and to diminish the others, to establish my mastery in "the unity of a world of masters and slaves" (RPH 71). This will to power is "an ideal that simultaneously brings with it its own form of universalization: war and conquest." (ibid.)

Conversely, I can suffer the aggression of another and become enslaved or exiled from my own place. My will and my consciousness are overwhelmed by the aggressor; my freedom immobilized or appropriated. There is the threat or infliction of physical pain or deprivation. This violence that I suffer is a burden for me, a submission that exceeds all my capacity to bear, a suffering at the heart of who I am. "For me" because I am personally set upon; I am destroyed. Such suffering isolates, absorbs consciousness, and, in rending one's own humanity, bespeaks a death before death - "unmakes the world", to use Elaine Scarry's phrase (Scarry 1985).

The third position of experiencing aggression is as a witness. Neither an attacker nor a victim, one is nonetheless immediately concerned with witnessed violence. It is a scandal! The vocation of witness is another subjection, another passivity, another imposition. It is not an issue of self-defense, as if a fight-or-flight instinct had been triggered. One needs to find out what is happening here. Who are these ones? What must I do?

"Witness" marks the bridge between sight and wisdom.[43] According to Oxford, witness is "knowledge, understanding, wisdom, the attestation of a fact" and a witness is one "who is or was present and is able to testify from personal observation" and as well from "the inward testimony of the conscience". The fact that is attested in the witness of aggression is that of a force wielded by one against another to move the latter against his or her will. It is a witness of violence. As a witness, my observation of aggression has to begin with its victim: if I don't understand that someone is being pushed around, I will not recognize that aggression has taken place. But if I am not directly involved in the situation - if my own interest is not at stake - how does this concern me? Why would I care?

Remember Levinas's comment on the position of the judge in *Otherwise than Being*:

> This means concretely or empirically that justice is not a legality regulating human masses . . . Justice is impossible without the one that renders it finding himself in proximity. His function is not limited to the "function of judgment," the subsuming of particular cases under a general rule. The judge is not outside the conflict, but the law is in the midst of proximity. (¶ 8)

What is true for the judge applies also to the witness. To be called to witness is to be called to consciousness and judgment "in the midst of proximity".

The evil of aggression collapses the distance of social space between the aggressor and the one aggressed against, and thus the annihilated victim has no recourse to language, no recourse to justice.

The testimony of a third-party witness reestablishes interhuman space in the world so that justice may be done.

persecutions and correspondences

The correspondences between these three experiences of aggression and the three movements of proximity are obvious. Aggression is like the approach of the Other. My experience of suffering and oppression is like being overwhelmed by the Other. And the experience of witnessing aggression is virtually identical to that of coming to consciousness in the presence of the neighbor's face, being "born unto the grief of the other". I have already alluded to this by describing the movements of proximity as the "an-archetypes" of aggression, resistance, and justice or ethics.

Other commentators (cf. Critchley 1999, Weber 1995) have remarked upon the strangeness of this juxtaposition of ethics and persecution - or proximity and aggression - in Levinas's work. Is the ethical subject necessarily a traumatized subject? Why would the figures of persecution be particularly appropriate to describe an ethics? Certainly, one of the questions that underlie my own attempt to use Levinas to understand justified violence is why it should be that persecution in the world enacts such a skewed reflection of the proximity of the other - because however counterintuitive these connections between persecution and ethics seem, they must be there. If Levinas believes that all human relations lead back to the peaceful order of proximity, there can be no ultimate dualism of good and evil. Further, it is the priority of an absolute or transcending Good that grants Levinas's emphasis on subjectivity proof against moral relativism, even if knowledge of the Good is itself open to skepticism. That being said, the correspondences between proximity and being apparent in aggression certainly warrant a closer look.

At first glance, the correspondence between the Other's approach to me and my violence against another could provide grounds to justify my own acts of violence. If the approach to me is persecutory and good, then why shouldn't I persecute another? But under scrutiny the correspondence seems to vanish like the Cheshire cat. One problem lies in the lack of the Other's presence. Aggression is an expansion of being. If the Other is "otherwise", how can there be aggression? A related difficulty is that, if the approach of the Other is irreducible, if it cannot be captured in a theme, it is not logical to speak of it corresponding with anything. "To speak" of a "correspondence": these are functions of consciousness. The approach, precisely, is not.

Paradoxically, it becomes easy to think of the approach as aggression just because consciousness, incapable of capturing what is so radically exterior to it, in the end fails to distinguish between being singled out in proximity and being on the receiving end of aggression. Face to face with the other, I am not free; I am constrained. How easy it is to compare that constraint to the limits imposed upon my freedom by those more worldly "powers that be", be they institutional powers or a local bully. How easy it is to think that the same result - the limitation of my freedom - derives from the same cause. Moreover, it is an easy mistake to want to make, just because of the second unfathomable anomaly of trying to accuse the Other of aggression: the more I try to think of the Other as an aggressor invading my own innerness, the more evident it becomes that it is I who have no justifiable claim for this place I occupy. It is easy to reject such a thought, to rather take the scene "at face value", to look at the face without attending to it.

At the same time, the correspondence between persecution in the world and before the face of the neighbor is quite exact. Levinas's description holds as well for both:

> Persecution is a trauma, violence par excellence without warning nor a priori, without possible apology, without logos. Persecution leads back to a resignation not consented to, and consequently crosses a night of unconsciousness. (197, n. 27)

In both cases, one's being - the freedoms of identity and capability - is devastated. The significant commonality between the approach and aggression is this devastation, being laid waste in a dark night of unconsciousness.

Proximity is diachronic, at once the time of the Same and the time of the Other. Subjectivity and the Face are the gates which both bind and separate the orders of being and proximity. At once both participating in and breaking through the grasp of perception, they occupy the excluded middle ground of the rationality of Being, not "either is or is not" but "both being and on the 'hither side' of being". It is in this way, face to face, that the relationship between the Same and the Other, between me and the neighbor, can be maintained without one being crushed by the other. What this modality cannot maintain, what it in fact implacably resists, is any idea of subjectivity that refers purely to self-interest, to being only in myself and for myself. The command of the face is disastrous for the egoic self, but beneath the accusation and persecution of this *cogito* or *conatus,* another meaning of subjectivity, as the-one-for-the-other, remains.

Aggression, on the other hand, resists proximity, insists on the here and now of subjective consciousness. It is the forcefulness of an intentional consciousness, of a being persevering in its being, duly directed by self-interest. In its everyday usage, aggression refers to a first strike, an unprovoked attack. In the aggressor's own experience, however, the very presence of another, a different other who cannot be accounted for, is already provocation. If perseverance in being is one's sole *raison d'être,* the simple presence of the unassumable difference of another challenges one's sovereignty in the world. The freedom of the other is a threat to one's own freedom. This threat requires attention, evaluation and action. What are her intentions toward me? How does his strength compare to my own? What have we each to gain or to lose? These attempts to encompass the other within a scheme of interest are already in the mode of aggression. If one then engages in force against the resistance of the other to this egoic imperialism, one may succeed in taking over the other's place, in establishing one's mastery at the cost of the other's freedom or even their life.

In this mastery, it is apparent that although the approach of the Other may not correspond with aggression, aggression may correspond with the approach - that is, with the substitution of the one for the other that is imposed by the Other in proximity. If that substitution is a "good violence", where exactly is the wrong in aggression? What distinguishes the two and how are they related?

Two things can be said about these questions. First, we should note that any such wrongfulness is apparent only to the eyes of a witness, a third party to the aggression. In the moment of action there is no problem for the aggressor, and the victim, silenced or annihilated, has no access to the distance required for judgment.

The second is perhaps a strange bit of fancy on my part, but one which keeps surfacing whenever I consider this problem. In an essay entitled "The Original Traumatism: Levinas and Psychoanalysis", Simon Critchley concludes that:

> Levinas seeks to think the subject at the level of the unconscious in relation to an original traumatism. The subject is constituted through a non-dialectical transference toward an originary traumatism. This is a seemingly strange claim to make, yet my wager is that if it does not go through then the entire Levinasian project is dead in the water. (Critchley 1999:239)

Without claiming any expertise in psychoanalytic theory, it seems to me that aggression can be understood in a way which both supports Critchley's reading of the subject in Levinas and perhaps lends the Levinasian project a paddle by demonstrating a link between proximity, trauma and aggression. I want to suggest that aggression serves the traumatized subject as an attempt to resolve the originary traumatism through repeating it and passing it on. The original trauma is the approach of the other that takes the subject hostage. One can't get hold of this violence by any means: it comes from nowhere, it has always already occurred but its time cannot be recalled. All that is certain is that one is inextricably obliged to the other. If that violence is not redeemed or expiated in the recurrence of subjectivity in substitution, if there were some impediment to the reduction of the egoic self to the responsible and irreplaceable *I*, it would indeed be unbearable. Without access to the Other, in whose service *I* am, there would be no refuge for the self in the world. I suspect that this impediment would lie in the interhuman order, such that the hapless subject is not welcomed as a legitimate other by the nearest others - more simply, is not received in the world with love. In such a situation, mightn't it be natural for this one to take up the role of the Other as it is perceived from the ego's position? Unable either to avoid or to respond to the call to divest oneself in place of another as the responsible one, the traumatized self simply takes the place of the other by force, taking another innocent one as hostage for one's own unspeakable innocence. If there is anything to this at all, aggression would be a terribly and tragically mistaken response to the simultaneous appeal of the proximate other and a profound betrayal of illeity at a social level.

Whether or not aggression is a pathological mistake, we have still not determined the nature of its iniquity. Unfortunately, once one stops taking the "badness" of violence as given, it becomes difficult to articulate exactly where the problem with aggression lies. It clearly must have something to do with the violation of someone's being, of their identity or capability. We humans are sentient creatures, vulnerable to trauma, to physical pain and other insults. The logic is simple. Pain is a vexed condition. Humans want to avoid it. If I inflict pain upon you against your will, I have done you wrong - as you surely have when you assault me. But it can't be that simple, because we've found that just such a violation of me by another can be a good thing. The real violence that is done to me and my freedom in proximity cannot be screened out or excused just because the violation is made ambiguous by the diachronic nature of the relation between me and the other. I suffer, against my will - and somehow I find it is good and right, also against my will. This is not the case in aggression.

This means that the evil of aggression cannot be fully accounted for by reference to the personal freedoms of will and identity. In Levinas's essay "Ethics as First Philosophy", he writes of "an immemorial freedom that is even older than being, or decisions, or deeds." (LR 84) This earlier freedom must refer back to the "older than" of the anarchic revelation of the Other and the hypostasis of the subject. It is this earlier freedom that provides the first ground for consciousness and all social relations. Perhaps the evil of aggression also comes back to this realm. Good and bad violence that cannot be distinguished in experience cannot either be differentiated in terms of being. Both violences are persecutory: both "lead back to a resignation not consented to", which is the resignation of the egoic self, and both consequently cross "a night of unconsciousness". The fundamental difference must be that *in the dark night of aggression that earlier freedom - the core of one's own significance - is violated and in the persecution of proximity it is not.*

This leads to a different understanding of the wrong of violence. Its wrongfulness is adjudged not just by the application of some universal principle about human rights and freedoms, but because of this prior freedom that supports one's access to the transcendental relation of the *I* to the Other which, in turn or again, is the platform of the interhuman. To violate that immemorial freedom is evil, pure and simple. Through injustice "all the foundations of the earth are shaken".[44] This violation leaves its taint in being, even if it cannot be isolated in consciousness, and it is in *both* the trace of this earlier violation of an older freedom and also always in the presence of those who suffer that our moral and legal codes and judgments are articulated.

the witness of aggression

The third experience of aggression is the role of the witness. In Levinas's scheme of things, justice is at issue in the very eruption of consciousness. Remember: if it was just me and the other, there would be no problem. In that anarchic archetype of the ethical relation, *I* am simply infinitely responsible before and for the other. But the entry of the third party, all the other others, occurs simultaneously with the turning of that face, and I am forced to measure my responsibility for the one in the sudden exigency for justice for all these other ones. This (proto-)experience describes the gateway in subjectivity between proximity and the world, at the furthest reach of proximity. The witnessing of aggression is this selfsame gateway, but at the furthest reach of being. They are virtually the same point.

In *Otherwise than Being or Beyond Essence*, Levinas speaks of conceptual possibilities that go beyond the possible, beyond "the rules of the game", such as:

> *substitution of one for another, the immemorial past that has not crossed the present, the positing of the self as a deposing of the ego, less than nothing as uniqueness, difference with respect to the other as non-indifference . . .*

In these significations, far from any game and more strictly than in being itself, men stand who have never been more moved (whether in holiness or in guilt) than by other men in whom they recognize an identity even in the indiscernibility of their mass presence, and before whom they find themselves irreplaceable and unique in responsibility. (58)

In these significations stands the I as witness, testifying not only to the truths of perception, but to the inward testimony of the conscience, and the "glory of the Infinite", by which the "infinitely exterior becomes an 'inward' voice, but a voice bearing witness to the fission of the inward secrecy that makes signs to another" (147). As a witness, I am moved by another. I am "born unto the grief of the other".

It is a persecution: as witness, I leave the world to serve the other. No longer I in the complacency of being myself, but I given over to the other because that is what I do. Given over in spite of myself, and so bereft even of the honour that is owed a hero. Impoverished, naked, like the companions of Job who rent their own clothes in despair and *sat down with him upon the ground seven days and seven nights and none spake a word unto him: for they saw that his grief was very great.* (Job 2:13) The witness is silenced, but it is a silence inspired by great awe or great shame. One is reduced to silence not by the forcefulness of the other - but by his suffering, and by the inability of gross being, with all of its *logos* and *nomos*, to find words of any use at all. One is reduced to silence, to less than nothing, until all there is to offer up is the expression of oneself, one's very inwardness given over as a sign and a pledge to the other: and in that resignation without consent, that pure saying without anything said, to find oneself thus "irreplaceable and unique in responsibility".

And so, in this phenomenology of suffering and witness we find the I and the other twined together in agonized silence. These are profoundly different silences - different resignations without consent, different nights of unconsciousness. As witness, I am silenced by being pulled out of the world into substitution or responsibility for the other, but the other is thrust out of the world into a single point of being, of pain, of suffering: aggression shatters the common space of language. And yet it is this senseless suffering of another, however much silenced and disappeared, that finds *me*, that penetrates my consciousness and proclaims to me my duty.

> Is not the evil of suffering - extreme passivity, helplessness, abandonment and solitude - also the unassumable, whence the possibility of a half opening, and, more precisely, the half opening that a moan, a cry, a groan or a sigh slips through - the original call for aid, for curative help, help from the other me whose alterity, whose exteriority promises salvation? . . . For pure suffering, which is intrinsically senseless and condemned to itself with no way out, a beyond appears in the form of the interhuman. (EN 93-4)

In the very impossibility of suffering to be borne, a space opens. A sound (a breath, a scream) slips through. The witness offers presence that the other may speak. Space, time, and communication are re-established, and the world begins anew in the form of the interhuman.[45] Here is the story of proximity and the signifying of subjectivity and the revelation of the other all over again.[46]

My earlier development of the moments of proximity described latent subjectivity awakening to a mysterious call (*yes?*). The distance between this one and the radically Other is infinite and diachronic. The relation is transcendent. Earlier than freedom, the subject is nothing but response to the call and the approach of the Other. *Me voici*. And then appears the third party as my neighbor and all the others for whom justice is necessary, who multiply and limit my responsibility and approach me for myself. And finally, under the weight of exigency, accusation and persecution, *here I am*, for-the-other, and with all the others, being capable and full of possibilities. And this one is always at risk of reification, of getting caught up in its own skin, of forgetting the immemorial Other.

The call to witness comes from someone who suffers, someone whose being has been assaulted, who has been expelled from the world. The call reaches to someone still in the world "whose alterity, whose exteriority promises salvation". For the one called, it is heard as from proximity (from elsewhere, and closer than a heartbeat) and complacency is troubled. The call is without force. For all its directness - and it comes, immediately and irremissably to *me* - it does not enforce itself because the call comes from "a dimension of transcendence whereby [the other] can present himself as a stranger without opposing me as obstacle or enemy" (TI 215). Responding to that call, under accusation, the ego is pulled out of being into the silent expressing of pure saying, the self given over to the other as a sign. Now there are two silences, two nights, of the one who suffers uselessly at the hands of an aggressor, and of the one who suffers for that suffering, and suffers as well the unconsented resignation of its own self for the other. Here, in "a breakdown of essence . . . a relaxation of essence to the second degree" (185), in the unassumability of this suffering, a crack appears in the darkness. After seven days and seven nights prostrate in the presence of grief, we begin to speak.

resistance and proximity

The final correlation between proximity and violence to consider is the approach of the other in proximity as the origin of resistance. *Re-sistere:* the root means "to stand"; the prefix signifies "doubling, repeating". According to Oxford, to resist is to hinder, to stop, to withstand, to stand against. Resistance is what aggression meets as it strikes out against the being of another. As pure sensibility before any action, it is immediate and responsive and profoundly personal. I am never so present within myself as I am when I experience the peculiar enigmatic approach of another. And yet, the signifyingness of resistance goes back to the offering of presence for the other in proximity, to the response to an approach in the pre-history of subjectivity. Returning to the root, and to the very redoubling or recurrence of the *I* to the *oneself,* resistance paradoxically signifies the taking up of one's being in consciousness and incarnation out of an irrecusable responsibility for the others, in inspiration or obsession by the other.

Subjectivity is both the term of a relation and the relationship itself. Its singular and defining relation is with some Other which is outside of or exceeds any thematization or system. The perseverance of this relationship, like any other, relies on both connection and separation. The approach of the Other comes like a call in the night to me: uniquely to me, myself evaded of any quality, a me that occurs only in this call. Such an occurrence, that immediate unmediated response in the night (*yes?*), is the anarchic origin of resistance. Here I am, immediately responsible for the connexity of the relationship, bound to be bound to the other, for the other. Resistance is what the Other encounters, a resistance incessantly and immediately surrendered and given over to the other, despite myself, because I cannot let the other alone. The Other, in its mode of illeity which is its own resistance to my approach, preserves the separation between us.

At the same time, being bound to the other brings me face to face with the third party which limits and expands my responsibility and obliges me to presence and thence to giving. Here, in the movement of desire and the resistance offered by the neighbor, is the good violence of creation. By the neighbor, the subject takes up being. This is the beginning of a linkage between resistance and violence.

In the order of being, the subject encounters two different resistances. It can be opposed in its *jouissance* by a physical resistance, where one's will or desire runs up against a force that opposes it. That opposition may produce in turn one's own force of resistance. The situation is weighed up, interests are considered (to the extent that what resists is capable of bearing interest). The matter is resolved (if at all) one way or another, by force or negotiation or by the surrender of one side or the other.

The resistance that I meet in the face of my neighbor, a purely ethical resistance, is absolutely different. "The expression the face introduces into the world does not defy the feebleness of my powers, but my ability for power." (TI 198) The face withstands my advance and my usurpation immediately by its being and by its alterity. In my freedom, I can turn all the world into my concern, my project, make it my own. All the world, but not the face of the other. *Il me regarde.* The face concerns me in its modality which, *qua* face, is otherwise than being. Absolutely resistant to "assemblage, conjunction and conjuncture, to contemporaneousness, immanence, the present of manifestation, [the *otherwise than being*] signifies the diachrony of responsibility for another and of the 'deep formerly', more ancient than all freedom, which commands it" (19).

The other opposes me without force, in a way which I cannot resist. I cannot pit my interest against the other's because the other's interest is already my own. I am disinterested - stripped of my interest just as "disinheritance" would strip me of inheritance. Without a struggle, I am surrendered. With this good violence which grasps me as the unique one and allows for no resistance, peace reigns in the order of proximity. It is incumbent on me.

However, the surrender of the ego is never final and complete but incessant, so long as consciousness is called for in justice for the other. The being of the other in its vitality and vulnerability requires the manifest presence of the subject. The ethical resistance disables "my abilities for power", but if my neighbor suffers with hunger or pain or homelessness, my responsibility requires that I take up that power again in order *to do something*: to witness, to understand, to give everything all over again. That resumption of power is then *resistere*, a resistance for-the-other. *In the resistance which stands against injustice resounds an echo of the offering of presence to the pre-original call.* This betrayal of the intimacy and peace of surrender is another violence, even as much as it happens for the sake of the neighbor's well-being, but subjectivity itself is expiation for this first violence of justice.

At the same time, because the other withdraws and leaves to me my freedom, the presence of the other in the turning of the face is the opportunity for the ego to once again take up with itself against the other. It is possible, even because one is obliged to attend to the corporeality of the other, to ignore that which signifies otherwise than essence. It is possible for resistance to harden into self-interest, indifference, and aggression. But - just because the other withdraws and leaves me to my freedom - it is also possible to offer one's presence to the other "on the brink of tears and laughter" (18), echoing the warm resistance of proximity, to surrender, to give oneself over to the other as the only original meaningful freedom, to be for the other:

> For subjectivity to signify unreservedly, it would be necessary that the passivity of its exposure to the other not be immediately inverted into activity, but expose itself in turn; a passivity of passivity is necessary, and in the glory of the Infinite ashes from which an act could not be born anew. Saying is this passivity of passivity and this dedication to the other, this sincerity. Not the communication of a said, which would immediately cover over and extinguish or absorb the said, but saying holding open its openness, without excuses, evasions or alibis, delivering itself without saying anything said. (142-3)

And so the approach of the other triggers my resistance which begins as sincerity, as a pure expression of my presence. Here I am. The relationship with the other is now one of co-presence, and therefore one of risk. The shared territory required for care and concern is exactly the shared territory required for violence and evil. Levinas's analysis of the other as the source of one's desire, the "neighbor" or the "beloved", is not meant to suggest that all of the people who approach us in a day do so with hearts brimming with lovingkindness for us or, for that matter, that we approach each one of them with full awareness of their uniqueness, their transcendence and nearness to us. Proximity, even as it continues to signify, can itself be resisted by the wills and powers of being. Here is a further link between resistance and violence. Murder is certainly possible, and even tempting, both for me and the others.

Resistance is my response to the approach of another towards me. It brings me to myself. Here I am. In the realm of being, the subjective experience of resistance - the self-reflexive experience of one's own presence - is also dichotomous. It can be "warm" and welcoming of the other, or it can be "cold" and self-interested, aggressive or fearful. Who approaches? Why and for what? What do they take me for? What are they to me? Following Levinas, it is clear that being myself crucially depends upon being approached by an other.[47] Like nothing else, the approach identifies me in election or accusation and brings me to myself.

This doesn't mean that I'm not going to be approached by other persons who get it wrong, who treat me as an extension of their own purposes, who seek to constrain my freedom, exploit my labour, persecute or oppress me. They approach with a forcefulness which is totally alien to the approach of the Other of proximity. They are mistaken. I will resist, if I am able, and oppose my force to their own. The immediacy of resistance in self-defense, defense of myself, is even earlier than an aversion to pain.[48] It is an ethical resistance, in refutation of an imposed and false identity: *I am not that*. Resistance can be so confident only if it is already established in its uniqueness as the-one-for-the-other, if it already signifies the diachrony of subjectivity and responsibility. Resistance is "the secret of joy" as an expression of this uniqueness in responsibility and election, as affirmation of a will and a freedom that is one's own and already otherwise pledged.

It is also possible that my resistance could be triggered by any opposition to my will, any impediment to my more avaricious desires. This is a case of "cold" resistance, simply a matter of opposing interests, of another skirmish in a world "turned over to the interplay and the mortal strife of freedoms". If "warm" resistance is presence offered to the other, "cold" resistance is presence staked against the other. The difference between the latter and aggression is minimal, if it exists at all. This is the final link between resistance and violence.

The key to the ambivalences of resistance - both encountered and expressed - is that it is always the immediate response of some one to the approach of an other. It isn't just that one is approached either by a friend to be welcomed or by an enemy to be resisted. One's very capacity to respond (to welcome, to resist) already signifies that, prior to consciousness and any memorable past, one is at the receiving end of an enigmatic approach which, in its consummate reticence or withdrawal, initiates the relationship which is one's very subjectivity; a relationship which is maintained by one's presence for the other, the "warm" resistance of just being present for another. The ambivalence of resistance arises from the transcendent nature of this relationship:

my presence doesn't enclose the relationship; rather, it is constantly disturbed by the alterity of the other.

Before "the exposure to the other . . . immediately inverted into activity", subjectivity is passivity. Before I work out which one is a friend to me and which one is an enemy, I am obsessed by the Other. The determination of who is my neighbor is *never* my business. The neighbor comes always as a stranger, always a revelation. Thus it may be that one is approached by this one who is known to be a friend, only to find oneself subjected to the "bad" violence that disrupts ethical relationship or to the urgent appeal of an exteriority which outstrips the mutuality of friendship. Or, in the midst of battle, that one who is an enemy may disclose the face of a neighbor and one finds oneself suddenly accused and at fault. Consider again Levinas's description of the encounter with the face of the other:

> The face with which the Other turns to me is not reabsorbed in a representation of the face. To hear his destitution which cries out for justice is not to represent an image to oneself, but is to posit oneself as responsible, both as more and as less than the being that presents itself in the face. Less, for the face summons me to my obligations and judges me. The being that presents himself in the face comes from a dimension of height, a dimension of transcendence whereby he can present himself as a stranger without opposing me as obstacle or enemy. More, for my position as *I* consists in being able to respond to this essential destitution of the Other, finding resources for myself. The Other who dominates me in his transcendence is thus the stranger, the widow, and the orphan, to whom I

am obligated. (TI 215)

The face which the other turns to me is an act of ethical resistance: resistant to reduction and representation, and ethical in not opposing me but letting me be, maintaining the vital relationship between alterity and being. For subjectivity, ethical resistance is to hear the irrevocable cry of the other and "posit oneself as responsible", to bear the unassumable other passively and despite oneself, to present oneself first of all in an "openness, without excuses, evasions or alibis, delivering itself without saying anything said". (143)

the resistances and violences of being

Resistance, as the response to an approach, is a social relationship that refers back, like a shunt, to the one-for-the-other of proximity. On the side of proximity, the pre-original approach of the Other that is found in the resistance of a latent subjectivity effects the "good violence" of creation. First, there comes the call and withdrawal of the Other, a violence (if it is one) that is redeemed by the goodness of goodness. Alterity elicits the anarchic offering of presence of the subject.

This pacific surrender is then challenged by the revelation of the face of a neighbor, the irruption of the third party for whom justice is necessary. This second instance of "good" violence which befalls the subject is expiated by subjectivity itself, in its return to itself in consciousness and egoity. In this response to the third party, subjectivity crosses through a "dark night of unconsciousness" into the realm of being, where the one comes together with the others as contemporaries in an order of powers and possibilities, wills and freedoms. There is thus a risk of different violences, and a context for different resistances.

On the other hand, as Levinas writes, consciousness itself "is resistance to violence, because it leaves the time necessary to forestall it." (TI 237) The *I* comes to consciousness under accusation and persecution, called into being by the complication to my responsibility that the entrance of the others brings about. Violence is imminent because I have been obsessed by the Other alone, and also because I cannot completely answer for or expiate for the relation between my neighbors. Consciousness is the reduction of diachrony to synchrony, to the time necessary to go from the one to the other, to ask, to speak, to present oneself in resistance to violence. Peace is incumbent on me and "is produced as this aptitude for speech" (TI 23), beginning always with the call for me to answer for myself, and to be accountable.

This realm of being and entities is at once the domain of communication but also the field of war, and the ethical resistance of proximity and the expiatory resistance of simple presence may not be sufficient in opposition to the violence of aggression and evil. If one's very being is tied around an imperative for justice and the incumbency of peace, what must be done "if one is not to abandon oneself to violence" (193 n. 33) in a cold world "turned over to the interplay and the mortal strife of freedoms"?

Bearing in mind all that has brought us to this point, I would like now to turn back again to the paradox of just war in which force is taken up in order to resist force, to the significations of justification and "the good fight", and to the question of what peace may come from struggle.

Chapter IV. "When I speak of Justice"

Q: *Does the executioner have a Face?*

E.L.: You are posing the whole problem of evil. When I speak of Justice, I introduce the idea of the struggle with evil, I separate myself from the idea of nonresistance to evil. If self-defense is a problem, the "executioner" is the one who threatens my neighbor and, in this sense, calls for violence and no longer has a Face. But my central idea is what I called an "asymmetry of intersubjectivity": the exceptional situation of the *I*. I always recall Dostoyevsky on this subject. One of his characters says: "We are all guilty for everything and everyone, and I more than all the others." But to this idea - without contradicting it - I immediately add the concern for the third and, hence, justice. So the whole problematic of the executioner is opened here; in terms of justice and the defense of the other, my fellow, and not at all in terms of the threat that concerns me. If there were no order of Justice, there would be no limit to my responsibility. There is a certain measure of violence necessary in terms of justice; but if one speaks of justice, it is necessary to allow judges, it is necessary to allow institutions and the state; to live in a world of citizens, and not only in the order of the Face to Face. (EN 105)

All of these pages have been in service of Levinas's "true problem", of questioning ourselves about how best to struggle against violence. All of this has been in return to the paradox of just war, to the significance of an ethical imperative to do the wrong thing, and the significations that underpin the formulae of western secular just war doctrine. All of this has been an approach to the possibly monstrous possibility of armed struggle as an act of love.

From Levinas, we find that to be oneself is to be in contact, in response, and that to be responsible is from the first to be present, to rise up, to offer presence to another. We also find a concept of "good violence" in which the subject is singled out in accusation and persecution, guilty of nothing but responsible nonetheless, and secured, as a hostage, by an "other". And we find that subjectivity - as ego, uniting same and other - expiates for that violence.

From Levinas, we understand that there would be no problem if I was ordered to the other alone: my responsibility for and before the other would be infinite, and that my responsibility for the other extends even to liability for the persecution the other does to me. He speaks of turning the other cheek to the smiter (49, 111, 145), without meaning any notion of supererogation: to be able to take responsibility for the fault of one's persecutor is not "above and beyond the call of duty", but is a basic human faculty. It is goodness, maybe even saintliness, but it is simply and essentially human.

But, as with any human possibility, a subject could assume responsibility for the persecutor only as an *I* in the presence of the "third party", all the others who regard me. As soon as we are in the realm of consciousness - of possibility, simultaneity, copresence, the interhuman - we are faced with all of the possibilities and problems of justice and evil. Justice is a problem for the one with infinite and conflicting responsibilities. It arises in disinterest and non-indifference to one's neighbors and calls forth consciousness, simultaneity and distance, an intersubjective or social world. The problem of evil is the problem of being, the possibility of a willful or unconscious ignorance of faces in which presence is no longer a substitution – in Levinas's sense – but an aggression, an assertion and an imposition. The question of justice then requires an active and attentive presence in resistance to the violence of aggression. I would suggest that the original call to justice corresponds to the sense of justification as righteousness, as *doing*-right, obligation, duty, responsibility - what one is bound to before any commitment made in living memory. I would further suggest that the second sense of justification as *making*-right, the retrospective declaration of rightness, accords with the *work* of justice, intentional acts which both respond to the approach of the others in proximity and seek to "introduce equality", to alleviate suffering and restore peace. The recuperation of the violence of this justice is more uncertain than the straightforward expiation of the hypostasis. Hence the need for themes and theories.

The criteria and assumptions of just war theory take on a new significance when considered in terms of social relations which depend upon what Levinas calls "the exceptional situation of the *I*". They take on a new solidity and seriousness as expressions of one's connection with and responsibility for the others, as support for the obligations revealed in the face of a neighbor.

just cause

Just war theory separates just and unjust violence but it doesn't have a lot to say about the nature of the wrong. After Levinas, we can say that what is wrong is the useless unbearable suffering of someone, the violation of a freedom or a vulnerability - but even more profoundly than this (which does not demean but aggravates the fever of that suffering), aggression severs the connection to the other by and for which one *is*. All the foundations of the world tremble at injustice. Therefore, no matter that violence must be carefully and cautiously wielded, resistance and restoration is necessary. This is what it means to speak of a just cause. The other is not to be left alone to his death.

Following the passage quoted at the top of this section, a Levinasian position (which may not be Levinas's[49]) on the justification of self-defense needs some clarification. To begin with, my responsibility is without limit with regard to the Other that grasps me in proximity. The same responsibility would hold, presumably, if I were alone in the world with one other who came as a neighbor to me, no matter how that other treated me. That this is not the case, and is in fact purely hypothetical, is due to the simultaneous arrival of the third party. Common time and shared terrain open the possibility of exchange of all kinds. We appear as bodies in motion acting upon one another.

The possibility for me to justly and justifiably do any violence whatsoever to someone begins when one of my neighbors threatens another of my neighbors "and, in this sense, calls for violence and no longer has a Face". Justly and justifiably because this is still in accord with the "asymmetry of intersubjectivity", the "exceptional situation of the *I*". It is not self-interested resistance, but is for-the-other. I am not acting in my own best interest, but am indeed putting myself at risk. At the very least, I give up my innocence and good conscience; at worst, I may fall into the executioner's hands. But by not refusing the cause of the other, I remain in contact and therefore correct.

Is it not possible for me to justly and justifiably stand up against another for my own sake, to resist a threat against my own freedom? What Levinas seems to be saying is that it simply is not, that self-protection has nothing to do with justice. However, a distinction has to be made between a retaliation that stands against the aggressor in pure self-interest - a cold resistance insignificantly distinguishable from aggression - and an ethical self-defense that is still in touch with proximity.

Does the one who threatens me have a Face? If not, if I simply strike back coldly, there really is no issue of Justice. It is pure exchange, measurable in terms of reasonableness or naturalness. The executioner and I are interchangeable, on the same footing. But this sort of justification, as we have seen, falters without access to a "better Good". It gets hard to tell the good guys from the executioners.

At the same time, I do cherish my life, my sensibility and enjoyment. It is simply wrong for anyone to do violence to me. The question is: why? It isn't so much a political issue, that my right has been offended. My hurt is too immediate to be a particular of a universal, or to be a contractual transgression - even though the law may certainly be offended as well. *I* live it, not as a human or a citizen, but uniquely and personally. *I* am set upon as surely as I am found by the approach of the other in proximity. The difference between the persecution of illeity and that of the executioner is that the executioner does not withdraw in his advance. His arrival comes to annihilate me. His force does not merely immobilize my power, it puts in question my connection with alterity. The executioner comes as a fury of being, an expansion that seeks to reduce all before it to itself. He insults me not just in my freedom and the integrity of my person, but somehow in my glory, which is never derived from me alone, but has been invested in me as responsibility for the other by the goodness that has chosen me before all freedom. This is the first and ultimate evil that can be done against me and it alone justifies my resistance, my faultless defense of a self that is produced between being and infinity.

My access to justification in defense of myself is also not just an arbitrary enrollment, but refers to being "an other for the others", approached "for myself". Beyond any innate drive for self-preservation, humanity and justice depend upon the gratuitous and unenforceable bonds of proximity and responsibility. When there is even one person who would take my part against aggression, who would be my champion - a someone who is also a neighbor to me - then self-defense becomes a facet of my responsibility. These are not reciprocal relations of exchange. It is not a case of "you watch my back and I'll watch yours". It is rather that this one has responded to my suffering and taken on my defense, thereby putting himself at risk of all the moral and physical hazards that come with fighting monsters. Because he is also my neighbor, my responsibility for him extends to the responsibility he bears for me. To get things right between us, I need to take back as much of that responsibility for my own defense as I can. I have to fight my own monsters, take my own risks.

If, on the other hand, it is my neighbor under threat, I am simply required to use the best force necessary for justice for him: the executioner "calls for violence and no longer has a Face". Here, Levinas endorses just war theory's contention that aggression justifies forceful resistance. If the executioner had a Face, I would not be able to lift a hand against him without fault. That's what having a Face means: "all the weakness, all the mortality, all the naked and disarmed mortality of the other can be read from it." (EN 232) It is because he threatens my neighbor that he asks for violence, loses face, and thereby the ethical resistance that forbids me to harm him.

At the same time, it is only "in this sense". If the executioner was completely faceless, I would no more have compunction removing him from the scene than I would prescribing antibiotics if my neighbor was suffering from a viral infection.[50] It is because the executioner still appeals to me as "another neighbor" that I am forced to make judgments about him and his intentions, to find out what has already passed between him and my neighbor, and especially, to limit the violence with which I resist his threat. There is no question but that I do wrong to the executioner - but there is no question that I can ignore the suffering of my neighbor. I am at every moment at risk of violating the contact of proximity, of becoming an executioner myself. It is thus much worse for me to do harm, to overstep the line in this situation, than it would be for my own freedom to be assaulted. At the same time, it is a risk I must run if I am to avoid "blanching in non-resistance to evil".

Asked whether an SS man had what Levinas meant by a face, he said: "A very disturbing question which calls, in my opinion, for an affirmative answer. An affirmative answer that is painful each time!" (EN 231) But he also wrote that "[r]egardless of the rights of love, one must always provide and keep warm a place for Hitler and his followers. Without a hell for evil, nothing in the world would have meaning any longer." (cited, Burggraeve 1981:18) And even though he acknowledges that justice, trembling "on the verge of possible injustice" (170), must be tempered with mercy, he does not exclude the possibility that the death penalty belongs as well "to the categories of justice" (EN 231). At the very least, this is a recognition that an option of force must be available if non-violent resistance or mercy is to be a meaningful choice. This is no sanction of punishment by the numbers (and certainly not of punishment as deterrence), but perhaps simply an acceptance that execution may, in extreme cases of cruelty, finally be the only way a judge, after due process and consideration, could fully respect the humanity of both the violated neighbor and the defaced executioner. This would by no means erase the stench of murder or immunize the responsibility for it which would remain with those who served and were served by that court, each by each.

just conduct and social warrant

Resistance is what aggression meets, but resistance refers back to the human presence offered to the approach in proximity. Resistance that responds to the forceless appeal and accusation of the other is the very justification of being, the doing-right despite oneself of expiation. The suffering or destitution of the other requires that resistance take form and act, but action is risky, uncertain, dependent on "chances or delays, and something like good or bad luck". Justice always bears an element of force, corruption and betrayal as it reduces proximity to being, but justice is also an act of love, the interruption of being by proximity, responsibility for the "absolutely other other". The use of resistance is justified, but its conduct is not infallible. The appearance of the third party introduces a limit and a problem. Hence the role of social warrant in support of this resistance to authorize and limit justification (even if it is always I who must answer in the end) - "if one speaks of justice, it is necessary to allow judges, it is necessary to allow institutions and the state; to live in a world of citizens, and not only in the order of the Face to Face." (EN 105)

Justice is only an issue in the complexities of the interhuman. Reason and science and laws matter because we live together, imperfectly. The special responsibility of an *I* requires systems, but systems develop and are sustained by and in community, in common with others. They require consent and consent carries obligation. The commonality of a community is the communal sharing, each by each, of responsibility for the systems which sustain it, systems which allow the work of justice to be done but which also necessarily disregard the alterity of a neighbor - as if each one here were bound to say "We are all guilty for everything and everyone, and I more than all the others."

Responsibility requires judgment which is a burden for the responsible subject. By judging that judgment, by making a declaration concerning its righteousness and its justness, a "true society" - composed of "associates in justice" (EN 35), "a configuration of wills which concern each other through their works, but who look one another in the face" (EN 20) - supports the subject by recognizing the cause of justice and authorizing and limiting the use of force in its service. Guidelines such as the criteria of "just conduct" in just war theory are proposed, debated, and adopted within a framework of law and reason: just war must be proclaimed by a legitimate authority;

it must be defensive and a last resort; the force of retaliation must not exceed the force of the aggression; non-combatants must not be targeted. Justification as social warrant in this way shares the burden of responsibility for the violence of resistance or retaliation. This is a good thing, but it is not expiation. It is not peace.

The force of justice is required, always and first of all, to maintain the connection between orders, all the unique relations of every one with their neighbors, the diachronic transcendence of being in proximity with alterity. Resistance begins anarchically before any beginning as a simple passive offering of presence, already in violence - but a "good" violence, a "force" of Goodness, which is nevertheless expiated in the confluence of *I* and ego in the self. The "force of goodness" - that is, just force - there becomes phenomenal, material, empirical. This force is always in danger of leaning too far into self-interest and severing the connection with the neighbor upon which everything depends, but in the interests of justice, it is a risk which must be run. Between the "good violence" of proximity and the "bad violence" of being extends the possibilities of a just violence which, however enigmatically, participates in both.

just violence

Resistance is different from aggression because it does not originate in me. It is a *response* that bears witness to a relation between me and another. It is a true relation insofar as both the separation and connection between us are maintained. In proximity, I am responsible for connection, for the movement (of Desire) toward and for the Other, while the Other both approaches as appellant and accuser and withdraws into its own alterity or infinity, a distance which I also love for the other's sake.

In resistance, which is a relation that takes place in the world, I am called to the other by the initiative of the other but my response takes place as separation. I stop and present myself in order to measure up the situation. Passivity reverts into agency. The other person may maintain the relation in presence and separation, or he may simply withdraw, or he may threaten the relation by attempting to crush or overwhelm my position. In the first case, the relation of these connected "exteriorities" to each other can be peaceful, as dialogue or eros. In the second, the relation is broken, but there may be no harm and no blame. It is only the third scenario, in which the other will not let me be, that calls for a more forceful resistance: no longer a simple presence but a presence in opposition to the freedom of that destructive or oppressive will. I am responsible for the force of my resistance. I, and no one else, can be called to account for it.

Here is the knife's edge. Forceful resistance is called for not simply in defense of oneself. If that were the case, everything would be relatively simple. In "a world turned over to the interplay and the mortal strife of freedoms", one could assert a claim on one's own behalf against the other and resolve it by whatever procedure was available within that system. This is simply not good enough when resistance is called for in defense of the relationship with the other that is subjectivity - that is, resistance not in the service of conflicting interests and limited resources, but in the service of infinite responsibility and substitution, in defense of humanness, of being-for-the-other. If the use of force severs that relationship, it violates its own purpose, its own significance. And yet, injustice must be resisted. Force is called for. It must be possible that resistance can act against the will of another and still somehow have its violence redeemed.

The first question would be: with whom am I in relation in this situation where forceful resistance is called for? Who is my neighbor? Who am I for, and who against? Remember that the neighbor chooses me "despite myself", always before I could consent or decline. It is a revelation. The face of my neighbor is turned to me as a purely and absolutely ethical resistance, without force of substance, as a command that I shall not murder. It is a resistance that does no violence to me - indeed it founds and justifies my own freedom in my response, my expression - and yet it

> paralyzes my powers and from the depths of defenceless eyes rises firm and absolute in its nudity and destitution. The comprehension of this destitution and this hunger establishes the very proximity of the other. (TI 199-200)

This resistance disarms and transforms without alienation, just as in the story of the father smitten by his newborn son. The effortless power of this ethical resistance is significant. The face of this beloved one doesn't call for force but for presence and care.

Someone who causes my neighbor to suffer, however, does call for my forceful intervention. The cry for help that breaks through to me at once binds me and orders my response. I cannot turn away without fault. If my neighbor suffers in her sovereignty and her freedom, I am implicated even though I have done nothing wrong. Because my responsibility to my neighbor is irrecusable, my intervention against the will of her "executioner" is justified and righteous. But finding that I am held accountable even beyond my intention in the presence of the third party, and not being able to answer completely for the relationship between my neighbor and the third, I need to measure my response. Already justified in its cause, it still must be justifiable in its performance if I am to avoid becoming an executioner myself.

Again, it is not that the third party, this one who is oppressing my neighbor, would appear as another neighbor to me by virtue of any universal principle or subsumption under a category. It is - despite myself and my allegiance to the other, and despite the loss of face that results from oppressing - another Face, another revelation of uniqueness and infinity, another purely ethical resistance opposed to my powers. This may seem complete nonsense or completely undesirable, but there it is. (If I was ordered to my neighbor alone, there would be "no problem".) One must act decisively, apply the necessary force with due care and diligence and wisdom. What has already passed between these two? What is due to each? There is an exigency for justice, for the introduction of equality into the world, and an exigency for peace, for the cessation of useless suffering, and for the peace between the orders which is always - has always been - my concern.

The force of justice continuously struggles to equal the righteousness of its origin. One must act decisively, but with due care - an elusive combination. Due care will rarely provide certainty or guarantees, but ready or not one must still act. Justice is necessary now, without delay, and will always come too late for some. If someone is suffering, there is simply no time for a neighbor, judge or witness, to make a unique judgment based on a full appreciation of the detail of the situation and its context. So we make shortcuts: we apply the lessons of similar cases, we develop rules and laws and judicial process and make these known far and wide. We develop moralities and ideologies in "due care", in lieu of perfect justice. We lay the groundwork for social justification, for the declaration that a particular use of force can or cannot be declared right and just. Standing on this social ground, we might congratulate ourselves for our capacity to administer justice, for our virtue, for the clarity of our judgment, for the technology by which we have managed our responsibility to our neighbors, for the beauty of the declaration of our right. And well we might. All of this may be necessary, but it is dangerous, dangerous work.

The danger, above all, is the repression of alterity, the leveling of transcendence, the betrayal of the sacred trust of human being. The danger is complacency, a loss of vigilance for the "secret tears" of the other which only an *I* is able to perceive.[51] It is reification, congealing all the myselfs and all the others into the categories of the totality: us, them, the guilty, the innocent, the good, bad, the ugly. Interests come to the surface, and depth - the origin of the significance of all this, the forceless and unavoidable ethical appeal of the infinity and alterity of this unique and beloved other - is mistaken for a mirage, a will-o'-the-wisp. Think of Ebenezer Scrooge trying to pass off the rattlings and ragings of Marley's ghost *(Business? Business? Mankind is your business!)* as just a bit of undigested beef.

This danger is as real for a liberation movement as it is for the regime against which it struggles. Ideology is necessary. It is necessary to analyze relations of power. It is necessary to identify the tendencies of allies and enemies. It is necessary to counter the false consciousness of oppression. It is necessary to plot strategy and tactics, to influence groups according to their interests, to attempt to predict and control the progress of history, to justify the violence of resistance. It is necessary to resist evil. But war is not at the beginning and politics does not arise to serve its own ends. At the beginning is the peace of proximity, ethics, the transcendent relation with the other that calls me to my responsibility, my subjection, myself. Resistance, as presence and as politics, gives force to the forcelessness or non-phenomenality of the good. This is necessary, but in all its crudeness and gravity, it will always be open to question, never as good as the good that inspires it. At best, it will be just: it will at least preserve the deep relation between one and another, assuage the suffering of the indigent, introduce equality, encourage peace.

just violence and goodness

After Levinas, it appears that violence is justified in the service of, and limited by, one's infinite responsibility before the faces that call for justice. The righteousness of the conduct of that force remains uncertain. Its sanction depends not so much upon the achievement of any foreseeable end, but on how it affects the enigmatic approach and proximity of a neighbor in his or her radical *otherness*, in that singularity which signifies otherwise than or beyond being.

There is still a connection to be made between just violence and resistance and joy. I have spoken of the danger of just violence, the risk it runs of becoming its opposite, but I have also spoken of justification so far in terms of necessity and exigency. What remains to be explored is the possibility of just violence, the force of justice actually getting it right, of its ability to restore peace after injustice. How is it possible that violence could be extinguished itself, leaving no embers behind to be fanned into retaliation? Beyond necessity, where will we find the *goodness* of just violence?

Justice moves enigmatically between the orders of proximity and being. If its potential for injustice comes from its attachment to being, its potential for good must derive from proximity. More precisely, if its potential for injustice comes from the reversion of proximity to being, its goodness must come from the interpellation of being by proximity. From the perspective of the self, attachment to being is activity and sovereignty, and proximity is passivity and subjection. Before the self takes up a perspective, the approach of the Other is accusation and persecution, prior to freedom, prior to any offense. This violence, indeterminable as it is, is redeemed by its goodness and is expiated in subjectivity. If just violence is ever to be good - not just "good enough" - it must have its own redemption and its own expiation.

The instrument of this expiation can only be an *I*, stripped of any concept, for-the-other, Levinas's hyperbolic "passivity more passive than any passivity". It is thus a bit misleading to say "[t]he forgetting of self moves justice." (¶ 9) Rather, justice is moved by the forgetting of self. Justice is moved, and opens - like a heart - to the one whose self has fallen away. If I have at first taken myself up in responsibility for the other, it is for justice for the others that this self has to be surrendered, even if it is immediately again taken up in responsibility. This is the "exceptional situation of the *I*": "Signification signifies in justice, but also, more ancient than itself and than the equality implied by it, justice passes by justice in my responsibility for the other, in my inequality with respect to him for whom I am a hostage." (¶ 5)

The call to awaken which comes from nowhere or "elsewhere", from the exteriority in which the other abides, is an outrage, a persecution, an accusation that fits me like a glove although I have done nothing to incur it. I *am* the impossibility of refusing the charge of the other. That is my declaration, my justification, my word, already pledged to the other before any word could be spoken. Before freedom, I am in thrall to the other and this is both violence and goodness.

With the enigmatic turning of the face "between transcendence and visibility/invisibility", I am called to presence, to present myself, to offer presence to my neighbor and my neighbor, bound to respond. As I take place in the world, it will eventually come to me (the incessant revelation announced by the purely ethical resistance posed in the face that turns to me) that my justification is no longer certain. This is what it means to be called into question. Justification depends upon the connection I am able to keep with this unique and extraordinary other, with the order of proximity. I am responsible for the well-being of my neighbor, because my neighbor depends on me, and I am responsible for the bridge between orders that depends upon the openness of my identity. My being is justified not in my deeds but in my subjection, which is being for the other as substitute or hostage, a second degree of responsibility and passivity, being responsible for the others' responsibility, even to liability for the evil done to myself. Substitute or hostage means expiation.[52]

On the final page of *Otherwise than Being*, Levinas writes:

> For the little humanity that adorns the earth, a relaxation of essence to the second degree is needed, in the just war waged against war to tremble or shudder at every instant because of this very justice. This weakness is needed. This relaxation of virility without cowardice is needed for the little cruelty our hands repudiate. That is the meaning that should be suggested by the formulas repeated in this book concerning the passivity more passive still than any passivity, the fission of the ego unto me, its consummation for the other such that from the ashes of this consummation no act could be reborn. (185)

The first relaxation of essence is, paradoxically, the hypostasis of the subject as the chosen responsible one. In the presence of all the others, the intimacy of that responsibility is both infinitely expanded and limited, bringing to the subject the powers of presence: sensibility, enjoyment, consciousness, will. This is a firming up of essence, necessary for justice and the fulfilment of one's obligation toward the other.

In the interests of justice, of introducing equality into the world, systems are necessary. By way of such systems, a social order is established. The social order provides the context for norms of behaviour: what is allowed and what is forbidden. The foremost of these will concern the regulation of the use of force, by both prohibition and authorization; regulations "at every moment on the point of having their center of gravitation in themselves, and weighing on their own account." (¶ 8) One has access to this justification as a citizen, as an "interested party" purely by reference to the social order. This is not a bad thing, but it leaves one uneasy, vulnerable to all the doubts about the goodness of justification that I mentioned in the first chapter. Declaratory or social justification does not expiate for just violence. It merely pardons it, excuses the justified one from punishment. At its best, it does so as a sharing of the burden of responsibility in the communion or solidarity of a "true society". At its worst, it is not justice at all, merely legalisation and calculation, unconcerned with and incognizant of the violence done in its name.

For expiation, which means atonement and reconciliation, a "second degree" of passivity is necessary. For the "good fight" to be good enough, for peace to come, one must - *I* must - be found to be responsible for everything, substitute and hostage, not because of what I have done, but by what I am, without good conscience, justified only by the always unwarranted and undue contact with transcendence, being grasped by the other. This suffering is unassumable, a disaster, an act of grace.

Levinas speaks of the second relaxation of essence as "weakness" and a "relaxation of virility without cowardice", speaks of "the fission of the ego" and its "consummation for the other such that from the ashes of this consummation no act could be reborn". It occurs, not solely in proximity of the neighbor, but in the presence of one whose will contends with mine. It is accomplished as a second degree of responsibility: liability for the one who persecutes me. It means offering up to another only the forceless force of a purely ethical resistance. It means offering my own face in substitution for the lost face of the executioner. It means using my freedom to give up my freedom to the other: "the fission of the ego" by the reversion of subjectivity to its earliest significance, prior to freedom or non-freedom, by freely surrendering to the violence of an aggressor. It is a confession of weakness by which proximity confounds being, without any heroism because without any attachment to identity.

"To tend the cheek to the smiter and be filled with shame" (111, Lam. 3:30), to resist not evil, to love one's enemies (Matt. 5:39-44) - this is surely the furthest extent of being for the other, perhaps dying for the other: drastic, last resorts, when all else has failed. But this simple willingness not to will is effected in every act of kindness, every humility or reticence, "the little cruelty our hands repudiate", "the little humanity that adorns the earth". Is it good enough if it fails to discourage aggression, if it does not serve to resist the evil done to one's neighbor? Of course not. Injustice calls for effective resistance. What is indicated - without providing any means whatsoever to preach martyrdom - is the affinity of just war with proximity, in its redemptive good and the joy of its resistance. If reason tries to account for this self-violence, it perverts it into a narrative of self-interest, but in the subject it is transcendence itself, the dedication of the one to the other in responsibility and substitution. The affinity of just war with proximity is not the justifiable violence I do to an enemy (that is its affinity with being), but the recurrence of subjectivity as inspiration, the other in the same.

> [T]o demand suffering in the suffering undergone . . . is not to draw from suffering some kind of magical redemptive virtue. In the trauma of persecution it is to pass from the outrage undergone to the responsibility for the persecutor, and, in this sense, from suffering to expiation for the other. (111)

Justice is concerned with equality, with peace for the nearest and the one far off. "The nearest and the one far off" can also refer to the orders of being and proximity. To keep that peace is "the exceptional situation of the *I*." *I am* for justice in a way which signifies differently than being for-oneself. The good of just violence, like the good of proximity which accuses me beyond reason, is its assault on my ego, privilege, self-satisfaction. This uncommon good is not the goodness of my suffering but the transformation of that suffering into exposure and expression and offering, a deeper freedom, consummation and expiation for the other. In the immediacy of its moment, pure experience or undergoing, it is *(yes)* something joyful, something like a sacrament.[53]

last words

The paradox of just violence is by no means resolved here. Violence remains both wrong and necessary. But, after Levinas, we can understand that the necessity neither arises from expedience in a war of all against all nor obliterates the wrong.

The "good fight" is disinterested, compelled by the suffering of injustice, fought in resistance to evil. You take up arms because you must, because you love your neighbors before their enemy, and because you are implicated in their suffering - not because you are good or righteous.

Armed struggle thus may be an act of love, but in seeking to give forceful expression to the purely ethical resistance of love, those who fight monsters risk becoming what they hate. To take up arms is, in a sense, to give up one's face: a combatant is a legitimate target.

(This is the abomination of conscription.) But even an enemy may reveal a face, a face which holds to you in relation, for which you are responsible. It is best to limit one's forcefulness to a minimum, for the other and for oneself, in order not to unnecessarily jeopardize this relation.

You are responsible for your own actions and intentions and also those that are beyond you: the actions and intentions of your comrades and of your enemies. How you deal with these responsibilities is important, but it will always be worked out in the event. This is the critical gap between the immediacy of ethics and the distance of ideology. To find the right act for any moment requires both spontaneity and preparation. Spontaneity is opposed to reification, and to dogma.

You are responsible most of all to the appeal and command issued in the defenseless Face of the other. Everything depends on this.

Justification does not erase the scandal of violence. It doesn't go back and close over the time of violence. At best justification signifies a co-presence, a communal witness of the burden of responsibility - but it in no way renders one's responsibility the less. The exceptional situation of the *I* is unrequited. *Peace then is under my responsibility. I am a hostage, for I am alone to wage it, running a fine risk, dangerously.* (167)

There are no promises here, no guarantees. No good conscience. All the words stammer into silence. Apology, apo-logos. Not the silence of annihilation, but a silence of vigilance, of attention.

What peace will come? A political peace where the equality of each is confirmed in the distribution and acquisition of goods of every kind? This is of course a deep dream of the struggle. But at the heart of that dream and that struggle - prior to it or beneath it - there is the absolute inequality of a responsibility without any corresponding right. The patience and equality of justice depends upon the acute uniqueness of subjectivity before the truly Other, upon the extravagance of love.

Appendix. Excerpt from *Otherwise than Being*

from *Otherwise than Being or Beyond Essence*. Emmanuel Levinas, translated by Alphonso Lingis. Martinus Nijhoff Publishers: The Hague, 1981. pp. 157 - 162

¶ 1.   We then have to follow in signification or proximity or saying the latent birth of cognition and essence, of the said, the latent birth of a question, in responsibility. Proximity becoming knowing would signify as an enigma, the dawn of a light which proximity changes into, without the other, the neighbor, being absorbed in the theme in which he shows himself. We have to follow down the latent birth of knowing in proximity. Proximity can remain the signification of the very knowing in which it shows itself.

¶ 2.   If proximity ordered to me only the other alone, there would not have been any problem, in even the most general sense of the term. A question would not have been born, nor consciousness, nor self-consciousness. The responsibility for the other is an immediacy antecedent to questions, it is proximity. It is troubled and becomes a problem when a third party enters.

¶ 3.   The third party is other than the neighbor, but also another neighbor, and also a neighbor of the other, and not simply his fellow. What then are the other and the third party for one another? What have they done to one another? Which passes before the other? The other stands in a relationship with the third party, for whom I cannot entirely answer, even if I alone answer, before any question, for my neighbor. The other and the third party, my neighbors, contemporaries of one another, put distance between me and the other and the third party. "Peace, peace to the neighbor and the one far off" (Isaiah 57: 19) - we now understand the point of this apparent rhetoric. The third party introduces a contradiction in the saying whose signification before the other until then went in one direction. It is of itself the limit of responsibility and the birth of the question: What do I have to do with justice? A question of consciousness. Justice is necessary, that is, comparison, coexistence, contemporaneousness, assembling, order, thematization, the visibility of faces, and thus intentionality and the intellect, and in intentionality and the intellect, the intelligibility of a system, and thence also a copresence on an equal footing as before a court of justice. Essence as synchrony is togetherness in a place. Proximity takes on a new meaning in the space of contiguity. But pure contiguity is not a "simple nature." It already presupposes both thematizing thought and a locus and the cutting up of the continuity of space into discrete terms and the whole - out of justice.

§ 4.   Thus one would understand, in proximity, in the saying without problems, in responsibility, the reason for the intelligibility of systems. The [158] entry of a third party is the very fact of consciousness, assembling into being, and at the same time, in a being, the hour of the suspension of being in possibility, the finitude of essence accessible to the abstraction of concepts, to the memory that assembles in presence, the reduction of a being to the possible and the reckoning of possibles, the comparison of incomparables. It is the thematization of the same on the basis of the relationship with the other, starting with proximity and the immediacy of saying prior to problems, whereas the identification of knowing by itself absorbs every other.

¶ 5.   It is not that the entry of a third party would be an empirical fact, and that my responsibility for the other finds itself constrained to a calculus by the "force of things." In the proximity of the other, all the others than the other obsess me, and already this obsession cries out for justice, demands measure and knowing, is consciousness. A face obsesses and shows itself, between transcendence and visibility/invisibility. Signification signifies in justice, but also, more ancient than itself and than the equality implied by it, justice passes by justice in my responsibility for the other, in my inequality with respect to him for whom I am a hostage. The other is from the first the brother of all the other men.[n.23] The neighbor that obsesses me is already a face, both comparable and incomparable, a unique face and in relationship with faces, which are visible in the concern for justice.

¶ 6.   In proximity the other obsesses me according to the absolute asymmetry of signification, of the-one-for-the-other: I substitute myself for him, whereas no one can replace me, and the substitution of the one for the other does not signify the substitution of the other for the one. The relationship with the third party is an incessant correction of the asymmetry of proximity in which the face is looked at. There is weighing, thought, objectification, and thus a decree in which my anarchic relationship with illeity is betrayed,[n.24] but in which it is conveyed before us. There is betrayal of my anarchic relation with illeity, but also a new relationship with it: it is only thanks to God that, as a subject incomparable with the other, I am approached as an other by the others, that is, "for myself." "Thanks to God" I am an other for the others. God is not involved as an alleged interlocutor: the reciprocal relationship binds me to the other man in the trace of transcendence, in illeity. The passing of God, of whom I can speak only by reference to this aid or this grace, is precisely the reverting of the incomparable subject into a member of society.

¶ 7.   In the comparison of the incomparable there would be the latent birth of representation, logos, consciousness, work, the neutral notion *being*. Everything is together, one can go from the one to the other and from the other to the one, put into relationship, judge, know, ask "what about. . .?", transform matter. Out of representation is produced the order of justice [159] moderating or measuring the substitution of me for the other, and giving the self over to calculus. Justice requires contemporaneousness of representation. It is thus that the neighbor becomes visible, and, looked at, presents himself, and there is also justice for me. The saying is fixed in a said, is written, becomes a book, law and science.

¶ 8.   All the others that obsess me in the other do not affect me as examples of the same genus united with my neighbor by resemblance or common nature, individuations of the human race, or chips of the same block, like the stones metamorphosed into men by Deucalion who, behind his back, had to collect into cities with their hearts of stone. The others concern me from the first. Here fraternity precedes the commonness of a genus. My relationship with the other as neighbor gives meaning to my relations with all the others. All human relations as human proceed from disinterestedness. The one for the other of proximity is not a deforming abstraction. In it justice is shown from the first, it is thus born from the signifyingness of signification, the one-for-the-other, signification. This means concretely or empirically that justice is not a legality regulating human masses, from which a technique of social equilibrium is drawn, harmonizing antagonistic forces. That would be a justification of the State delivered over to its own necessities. Justice is impossible without the one that renders it finding himself in proximity. His function is not limited to the "function of judgment," the subsuming of particular cases under a general rule. The judge is not outside the conflict, but the law is in the midst of proximity. Justice, society, the State and its institutions, exchanges and work are comprehensible out of proximity. This means that nothing is outside of the control of the one for the other. It is important to recover all these forms beginning with proximity, in which being, totality, the State, politics, techniques, work are at every moment on the point of having their center of gravitation in themselves, and weighing on their own account.

¶ 9.   In no way is justice a degradation of obsession, a degeneration of the for-the-other, a diminution, a limitation of anarchic responsibility, a neutralization of the glory of the Infinite, a degeneration that would be produced in the measure that for empirical reasons the initial duo would become a trio. But the contemporaneousness of the multiple is tied about the diachrony of two: justice remains justice only in a society where there is no distinction between those close and those far off, but in which there also remains the impossibility of passing by the closest. The equality of all is borne by my inequality, the surplus of my duties over my rights. The forgetting of self moves justice. It is not then without importance to know if the egalitarian and just State in which man is fulfilled (and which is to be set up, and especially to be maintained) proceeds from a war of all against all, or from the irreducible responsibility of the one for all, and if it can do without [160] friendships and faces. It is not without importance to know that war does not become the insaturation of a war in good conscience. It is also not without importance to know, as far as philosophy is concerned, if the rational necessity that coherent discourse transforms into sciences, and whose principle philosophy wishes to grasp, has thus the status of an origin, that is, origin of self, of a present, a contemporaneousness of the successive (the work of deduction), the manifestation of being - or if this necessity presupposes a hither side, a pre-original, a non-presentable, an invisible, and consequently a hither side not presupposed like a principle is presupposed by the consequence of which it is synchronous. This anarchic hither side is borne witness to, enigmatically, to be sure, in responsibility for the others. Responsibility for the others or communication is the adventure that bears all the discourse of science and philosophy. Thus this responsibility would be the very rationality of reason or its universality, a rationality of peace.

¶ 10.   Consciousness is born as the presence of a third party. It is in the measure that it proceeds from it that it is still disinterestedness. It is the entry of the third party, a permanent entry, into the intimacy of the face to face. The concern for justice, for the thematizing, the kerygmatic discourse bearing on the said, from the bottom of the saying without the said, the saying as contact, is the spirit in society. And it is because the third party does not come empirically to trouble proximity, but the face is both the neighbor and the face of faces, visage and visible, that, between the order of being and of proximity the bond is unexceptionable. Order, appearing, phenomenality, being are produced in signification, in proximity, starting with the third party. The apparition of a third party is the very origin of appearing, that is, the very origin of an origin.

¶ 11.   The foundation of consciousness is justice. Not that justice makes a preexisting meditation intervene. An event like meditation - synchronization, comparison, thematization - is the work of justice, an entry of the diachrony of proximity, of the signifyingness of saying into the synchrony of the said, a "fundamental historicity" in the sense of Merleau-Ponty. It is the necessary interruption of the Infinite being fixed in structures, community and totality.[n.25] Synchronization is the act of consciousness which, through representation and the said, institutes "with the help of God," the original locus of justice, a terrain common to me and the others where I am counted among them, that is, where subjectivity is a citizen with all the duties and rights measured and measurable which the equilibrated ego involves, or equilibrating itself by the concourse of duties and the concurrence of rights. But justice can be established only if I, always evaded from the concept of the ego, always desituated and divested of being, always in non-reciprocatable relationship with the other, always for the other, can [161] become an other like the others. Is not the Infinite which enigmatically commands me, commanding me and not commanding, from the other, also the turning of the I into "like the others," for which it is important to concern oneself and take care? My lot is important. But it is still out of my responsibility that my salvation has meaning, despite the danger in which it puts this responsibility, which it may encompass and swallow up, just as the State issued from the proximity of the neighbor is always on the verge of integrating him into a we, which congeals both me and the neighbor. The act of consciousness would thus be political simultaneousness, but also in reference to God, to a God always subject to repudiation and in permanent danger of turning into a protector of all the egoisms.

¶ 12.   The pre-original, anarchic saying is proximity, contact, duty without end, a saying still indifferent to the said and saying itself without giving the said, the-one-for-the-other, a substitution. It requires the signification of the thematizable, states the idealized said, weighs and judges in justice. Judgments and propositions are born in justice, which is putting together, assembling, the being of entities. Here with a problem begins the concern for truth, for the disclosure of being. But it is for justice that everything shows itself, and to the extravagance of substitution is superimposed, through the exigencies for responsibility itself which substitution is, a rational order, the ancillary or angelic order of justice, and the very fact of seeing, seeing everywhere clearly and recounting everything.

¶ 13.   The way leads from responsibility to problems. A problem is posited by proximity itself, which, as the immediate itself, is without problems. The extraordinary commitment of the other to the third party calls for control, a search for justice, society and the State, comparison and possession, thought and science, commerce and philosophy, and outside of anarchy, the search for a principle. Philosophy is this measure brought to the infinity of the being-for-the-other of proximity, and is like the wisdom of love.

¶ **14.**   But, come out of signification, a modality of proximity, justice, society and truth itself which they require, must not be taken for an anonymous law of the "human forces" governing an impersonal totality.

¶ **15.**   It is through its ambivalence which always remains an enigma that infinity or the transcendent does not let itself be assembled. Removing itself from every memorable present, a past that was never present, it leaves a trace of its impossible incarnation and its inordinateness in my proximity with the neighbor, where I state, in the autonomy of the voice of conscience, a responsibility, which could not have begun in me, for freedom, which is not my freedom. The fleeting trace effacing itself and reappearing is like a question mark put before the scintillation of the ambiguity: an infinite responsibility of the one for the other, or the signification [162] of the Infinite in responsibility. There is an ambiguity of the order that orders to me the neighbor who obsesses me, for whom and before whom I answer by my ego, in which being is inverted into a substitution, into the very possibility of gift - and of an infinite illeity, glorious in the human plot hatched in proximity, the subversion of essence into substitution. In it I could not arise soon enough to be there on time, nor approach without the extraordinary distance to be crossed augmenting before every effort to assemble it into an itinerary. Illeity overflows both cognition and the enigma through which the Infinite leaves a trace in cognition. Its distance from a theme, its reclusion, its holiness, is not its way to effect its being (since its past is anachronous and anarchic, leaving a trace which is not the trace of any presence), but is its glory, quite different from being and knowing. It makes the word God be pronounced, without letting "divinity" be said. That would have been absurd, as though God were an essence (that is, as though he admitted the amphibology of being and entities), as though he were a process, or as though he admitted a plurality in the unity of a genus. Does God, a proper and unique noun not entering into any grammatical category, enter without difficulties into the vocative? It is non-thematizable, and even here is a theme only because in a said everything is conveyed before us, even the ineffable, at the price of a betrayal which philosophy is called upon to reduce. Philosophy is called upon to conceive ambivalence, to conceive it in several times. Even if it is called to thought by justice, it still synchronizes in the said the diachrony of the difference between the one and the other, and remains the servant of the saying that signifies the difference between the one and the other as the one for the other, as non-indifference to the other. Philosophy is the wisdom of love at the service of love.

---

n.23 Cf. *infra*, Chapter V, 2.

n.24 Here one has to denounce the suspicion that objectivism casts over all philosophy of subjectivity, and which consists in measuring and controlling the ego by what is objectively observable. Such a position is possible, but arbitrary. Even if the ego were but a reflection forming an illusion and contenting itself with false semblances, it would have a signification of its own precisely as this possibility of quitting the objective and universal order and abiding in itself. Quitting the objective order is possible in the direction of a responsibility beyond freedom as well as toward the freedom of responsibility of play. The ego is at the crossroads. But to quit the objective order, to go in oneself toward the privatissime of sacrifice and death, to enter upon the subjective ground, is not something that happens by caprice, but is possible only under the weight of all the responsibilities.

n.25 Thus theological language destroys the religious situation of transcendence. The infinite "presents" itself anarchically, but thematization loses the anarchy which alone can accredit it. Language about God rings false or becomes a myth, that is, can never be taken literally.

Bibliography

Blanchot, Maurice. *The Writing of the Disaster.* Ann Smock, trans. University of Nebraska Press: Lincoln and London. 1995.

Burggraeve, Roger. "The Ethical Basis for a Humane Society" in *Emmanuel Levinas,* Catherine Vanhove-Romanik, trans. Center for Metaphysics and Philosophy of God, Institute of Philosophy: Leuven. 1981.

Critchley, Simon. "The Original Traumatism: Levinas and Psychoanalysis" in *Questioning Ethics: Contemporary Debates in Philosophy,* Richard Kearney and Mark Dooley, eds. Routledge: London, New York. 1999.

Durcan, Paul. *A Snail in My Prime: New and Selected Poems.* Penguin Books: UK. 1995.

Feldmár, Andrew. "Dr. Love and Mr. Death: What Do Men Desire?", unpublished discussion paper read in Vancouver, 2000. (Philosophers' Café, sponsored by the Interdisciplinary Programs in Continuing Studies at Simon Fraser University)

Gibbs, Robert. *Correlations in Rosenzweig and Levinas.* Princeton University Press: New Jersey. 1992.

Harvey, Andrew. *The Essential Mystics*. Harper Collins Publishers: New York. 1996.

Kgositsile, Keorapetse. "Red Song", *When the Clouds Clear*. COSAW: Fordsburg, South Africa. 1990.

Kunz, George. *The Paradox of Power and Weakness: Levinas and an Alternative Paradigm for Psychology*. State University of New York Press: Albany. 1998.

Levinas, Emmanuel:

Alterity and Transcendence, Michael B. Smith, trans. Columbia University Press: New York. 1999. [AT]

Entre Nous: On Thinking-of-the-Other, Michael B. Smith and Barbara Harshav, trans. Athlone Press: London. 1998. [EN]

The Levinas Reader, Seán Hand, ed. Blackwell: Oxford and Cambridge. 1989. [LR]

Of God Who Comes to Mind, Bettina Bergo, trans. Stanford University Press: Stanford. 1998. [OG]

Otherwise than Being or Beyond Essence, Alphonso Lingis, trans. Martinus Nijhoff Publishers: The Hague. 1981. [( )]

"Reflections on the Philosophy of Hitlerism" [1934], *Critical Inquiry 17, Autumn 1990*. University of Chicago. [RPH]

Totality and Infinity: An Essay on Exteriority, Alphonso Lingis, trans. Duquesne University Press: Pittsburgh. 1969. [TI]

Nietzsche, Friedrich. *Beyond Good and Evil*. R.J. Hollingdale, trans. Penguin Books: UK. 1975.

Scarry, Elaine. *The Body in Pain: The Making and Unmaking of the World*. Oxford University Press: New York. 1985.

Shah, Indries. *The Way of the Sufi*. Penguin Books: UK. 1974.

Walker, Alice. *Possessing the Secret of Joy*. Vintage Books: London. 1992.

Walzer, Michael. *Just and Unjust Wars: A Moral Argument with Historical Illustrations*. Basic Books: New York. 1977.

Weber, Elisabeth. "Persecution in Levinas's *Otherwise Than Being or Beyond Essence*", Mark Saatjian, trans., in *Ethics as First Philosophy: The Significance of Emmanuel Levinas for Philosophy, Literature and Religion*, Adriaan T. Peperzak, ed. Routledge: New York and London. 1995.

Notes

* (*Otherwise than Being or Beyond Essence*, 177)

1 Does Levinas single out us Westerners because we are the inheritors of the political ideals of freedom and democracy? Or of the biblical values of love and humility? Or because it is a certain Western philosophy, lieged to reason and the love of wisdom, that will be challenged in this questioning? Or because we have been responsible for wreaking so much havoc in the world? Or perhaps he simply recognizes that one has to start from where one finds oneself. Sure.

2 All dictionary references are to the Shorter Oxford English Dictionary, 3rd edition, revised.

3 In fact, Walzer (1977:52) finds the wrong of aggression precisely in this authorization or invocation of violent response.

4 The implicit risk of injustice here is acknowledged in just war theory's insistence on "legitimate authority". Islamic scholars who challenged the justifiability of the attacks on New York and Washington in 2001 did so partially in terms of the same concept in sharia law.

5 Equity, including the possibility of a justifiable use of defensive force, can then be extended to include persons solely on the basis of their humanity before or beyond social position - at least, insofar as that humanity is recognized. The universality of natural human rights is curtailed when a social judiciary reserves the right both to attribute competency and to exclude the incompetent, whether children or women, criminals, slaves, the mad ones or the poor ones.

6 It is well said that "Self-justification is worse than the original offense." (Shah 1974:153)

7 Appendix.

8 "In metaphysics a being separated from the Infinite nonetheless relates to it, with a relation that does not nullify the infinite interval of the separation - which thus differs from every interval. In metaphysics a being is in a relation with what it cannot absorb, with what it cannot, in the etymological sense of the term, comprehend." (TI 80)

9 It may be important to note here that Levinas's work does not take "the Infinite" as an *a priori* principle or condition. The Infinite, or the transcendent, or God, is what "comes to mind" somehow in the concreteness of situations where what is not like being - what is beyond being or "otherwise than being" - makes itself felt in a manner that refuses to be reduced to a theme or an object of consciousness. Thus, in this revelation of subjectivity in proximity, Levinas states that the "transcendence of the revelation lies in the fact that the 'epiphany' comes in the saying of him that received it" (149) and that the "active source of this passivity is not thematizable" (111).

10 More imperatively, a scream, speech after the disaster, an interrogative that reveals both the presence of the one who asks and the dire absence of the one who is addressed, as in Gibbs' discussion of the Hebrew *mi yiten* in Rosenzweig's *Star of Redemption*: "This question expresses a wish, a wish that the one asked for were actually present. It asks for an absent actor ... most often God ... a questioning of faith, marked by a form of despair, but it does not abandon the hope for the dialogue. In place of the question that seeks an interlocutor in a certain kind of innocence, this is the question of the betrayed, of the survivor." (Gibbs 1992:103)

11 See Translator's note OG 202 (n. 7) for a similar treatment.

12 With Levinas, "produce" can be always taken in both its verbal senses - to cause or make and to bring forth.

13 This will receive a fuller treatment below.

14 I may seem to be diverging here from Levinas's description which finds that the reversion to consciousness is due to the possibility of the neighbor's guilt before the third party and the ensuing need for justice (193 n.29; AT 101), but elsewhere he also speaks of "the extraordinary commitment of the other to the third party"(¶13). Any possibility of the neighbor's guilt must refer first to this prior commitment, and it is this obligation of his for which I cannot answer.

15 This is an immanent critique of a sort, after Levinas. I accept his map of the territory which passes into proximity from the interruption of the concrete situation of being, in order to try to sketch another projection, to ask if you can get here from there. It is an altogether unlikely exercise, considering that proximity stretches out beneath and beyond the labours of any topology, offers no place from which to embark, is always already underway or passed.

16 "My presence does not respond to the extreme urgency of the assignation. I am accused of having delayed." (88-9) "This exigency with regard to oneself without regard for what is possible, that is, beyond all equity, is produced in the form of an accusation preceding the fault, borne against oneself despite one's innocence." (113)

17 Like the substitution of the-one-for-the-other, this is not a substitution of one thing that takes the place of another thing, nor is it a becoming that simply marks a change from one state to another: the face is both stateless and sovereign. Rather, it is *sub-stitution* - the neighbor present before me in its command or beneath me in its destitution, and *be-coming*, a coming-to-be, an approach that is well-come, immanent and imminent.

18 "[T]his poverty and exile which appeal to my powers, address me,

do not deliver themselves over to these powers as givens, remain the expression of the face."(TI 213)

19 This movement is related to that of illeity. I repel the other and the other withdraws. "The delay is irrecuperable. 'I opened . . . he had disappeared.'"(88)

20 This question of the goodness of creation and the "goodness" of the persecution which the other deals me is integral to the question of justification and will be more fully considered in the next chapter.

21 My terminology diverges somewhat from Levinas's here. He tends to double up "the neighbor" as both the Other in proximity and the other in the world to highlight their nearness, while the "third party" stands for all the other different others. I want to double up the "third party" as both the neighbor and the others to accentuate the being of the neighbor and the alterity of the Other. The enigmatic nature of the neighbor, both proximate and present, allows for either strategy without guaranteeing the stability of either. Levinas's risks allowing difference to be mistaken for alterity, while mine is in danger of making too extreme a distinction between them. Perhaps keeping both alternatives in mind will approximate a balance. Ultimately, the other and the Other can neither be fully separated nor compared.

22 When asked how to determine the exact moment of dawn, the rabbi in a Hasidic tale replies that it is then "when you can look into the face of a human being and you have enough light to recognize in him your brother. Up until then it is night and darkness is still with us." (in Kunz 1998:epigraph)

23 "Any man's death diminishes me, for I am involved in mankind." (Donne.)

24 "The "this as that" is not lived; it is said." (35)

25 In a similar tone, Levinas speaks of the "dehiscence" of proximity (84), a botanical term for the *bursting open* of a seed pod in order to discharge its mature contents.

26 This does not come about in the same manner as a qualitative dialectical change occurring within a system or totality. This third is not a negation of the approach, and no synthesis is accomplished.

27 "To be on the ground of the signification of an approach is to be *with another* for or against a third party, with the other and the third party against oneself, in justice."(16)

28 "The immemorial past is intolerable for thought. Thus there is an exigency to stop: *anagkè stenai.*" (199, n. 21)

29 "The intellect says: 'The six directions are limits: there is no way out.' Love says: 'There is a way: I have travelled it thousands of times.'" (Rumi, in Harvey 1996:156)

30 This inclusion allows for the bureaucracy of a state to deal with us impersonally, for better or worse. This is one of the meanings of "giving the self over to calculus" (¶7).

31 Privilege can of course be justifiable in circumstances where the law is seen to be not good enough, but such consideration requires consciousness, and is already an act of justice.

32 Someone might complain that this father's story involves direct kinship and cannot serve well as an analogy for a more distant encounter. I would reply that we are moved and caught up as well by the plight of those who suffer beyond the range of our vision, by those ones who face us even though we may never see them or know them by name. The point is that my responsibility to the other, no matter how close or far-off, always precedes and extends beyond the scope of my awareness or choice. The example of the father's response to his children is

simply more familiar to thought because there is a relation between them through both the commonness of "blood" *and* the exteriority of proximity. Even the closest family relationships are not completely reason-able, cannot be reduced to biology. The child is both my child and a stranger. The stranger also concerns me.

33 I use the term "work" in the following sense: "[It should be noted that Levinas's use of the term *oeuvre* often denotes (as here) a movement toward the other that does not return to the same.]" (EN 236, n. 4, translator's note) In French, it is *oeuvre* opposed to *travail,* a distinction that seems based on the compensation that does or does not return to the one who produces the work. The lack of return on one's *oeuvre* would not be an exploitation or alienation.

34 Here is Levinas at his most provocative. But he is identifying evil not with being *per se,* as if matter and life itself were evil, but rather with the unambiguous *order* of being which cannot allow for the precedence of the other and the "otherwise than being", and which therefore reduces the significance of human consciousness to merely human being.

35 "Conversation: the action of living or having one's being *in* or *among*; an interchange of thought and words". (OED)

36 Making a similar point in a different context, Levinas disputes both vengeance and forgiveness as means to end violence. "Such a rectification does not put an end to violence: evil engenders evil and infinite forgiveness encourages it. Such is the march of history." (EN 37)

37 "The passivity of the subject in saying ... is an offering oneself which is not even assumed by its own generosity, an offering oneself that is a suffering, a goodness despite oneself."(54)

38 "Ego" is both the conscious "I" of tautological identity (70),

complacent in its sensible enjoyment (73), and also behither that identity, the "one" of "oneself" where there is a noncoincidence in the reflection, or the site/non-site where non-sense overflows sense. (73-4) "The ego is an incomparable unicity; it is outside of the community of genus and form, and does not find any rest in itself either, unquiet, not coinciding with itself."(8)

39 "For the Good can not enter into a present nor be put into a representation. But being Good it redeems the violence of its alterity, even if the subject has to suffer through the augmentation of this ever more demanding violence." (15)

40 This breaking-into is like a violence of one's own birth. It is a trauma, outside of language, nocturnal, completely irrecuperable, a pure passage or interval. There can be no witness.

41 There is an oddness here. Just as the approach of the Other is in one moment both violent and in the absence of anything to violate, so we speak here of the rupture by the Face, of a subject that is already, before dialogue or intentionality, bound to the other. And yet, the revelation or accusation of the face is still a violence just because subjectivity is also bound to consciousness. Thus Levinas speaks of subjectivity, structured as being-for-the-other, doubly-bound, as a Gordian knot that can be sliced through, but never untied. (cf. 25, 77,105, 170)

42 The future also comes to me from "wherever". Like the Other, it never arrives or at least "I never saw it coming!". Unlike my death, I survive the future's continuous passage. Is time the Other? Is the Other the future? This is an idea that Levinas comes around to regularly but, I am relieved to admit, one which is beyond the scope of this study.

43 Through the common Indo-European root *wid-*, witness is cognate

with both vision (L. *videre*) and wisdom (OE. *wis-* to make known). The same root yields *veda* (knowledge) in Sanskrit, and, incidentally, the Greek gives to *wise* the sense of "manner or mode", as in "otherwise than being". Wisdom is the link between being and goodness.

44 Perhaps God comes to mind when one attempts to take in the enormity of this: "What God has put together, let no man put asunder." To offend another is to offend God.

45 This is perhaps affirmed in the Talmudic claim that "he who saves a single life, saves the world entire." (Tractate Sanhedrin)

46 Does the pathology of traumatic neurosis, described by Critchley as unconscious and compulsive repetition of the trauma, mimic this? Could the drive to psychological integrity after the annihilation from persecution be resolved in an openness to the other, being-for-the-other? We would need to find understandings of subjective integrity and annihilation which reach beyond the boundaries of reductive psychology.

47 In South Africa, recognition of this was inscribed in the interim national constitution as *ubuntu*, the Xhosa word for the quality of being human. This concept is often expressed in English as "I am because we are" - a phrase with a certain Levinasian ring to it.

48 It must be remembered that the *active expression* of resistance in human society, as opposed to this subjective "immediacy", is also a function of political consciousness and relations of power. Resistance in the defense of one's interest is only likely for those who understand they have an interest to defend. For example, a resistance to oppression might indeed require mediation and development, such as "consciousness-raising" or political education, but this is already founded on an earlier and immediate worth or presence prior to any "free attitude

toward value that could be taken up" (198 n.28).

49 As will be shown in the following discussion, it seems to me that "the problematic of the executioner" can indeed open - and is even more complicated - "in terms of a threat that concerns me". However, since I find that it "concerns me" in my involvement with the other in proximity, I believe I am still fundamentally in accord with Levinas.

50 Should I worry about my lack of compassion for the life force of a bacillus? Where does one draw the line on responsibility to other species and genera? Judgment, as always, is necessary - but any such compassion for other forms of life could only be an act of consciousness, imagination, and generalization, and as such would likely refer back eventually to one's passivity and subjection under the direct and immediate appeal of a human face.

51 "There are, if you will, tears which a state functionary cannot see: the Other's tears . . . In such a situation (of the socio-political order) individual consciences are needed, for they alone are able to perceive the violence which proceeds from the proper functioning of Reason itself." (Levinas [*Transcendance et hauteur*], cited in Burggraeve 1981: 52)

52 "To transcend oneself, to leave one's home to the point of leaving oneself, is to substitute oneself for another. It is, in my bearing of myself, not to conduct myself well, but by my unicity as a unique being to expiate for the other." (182)

53 In words it is merely ridiculous, a setup for suspicions of cant and hypocrisy. So it goes, and just as well. The inability of the said to contain such sincerity is its saving grace. Cf. appendix, n.25

Photo by: Basil Breakey

Helen Douglas has published widely on Levinas, philosophical counseling and "everyday philosophy". She has a counseling practice in Cape Town, South Africa, where she lives with her husband Rob.

www.ingramcontent.com/pod-product-compliance
Lightning Source LLC
Chambersburg PA
CBHW021333090426
42742CB00008B/595